BUS

YEARBOOK-10
Edited by Gavin Booth

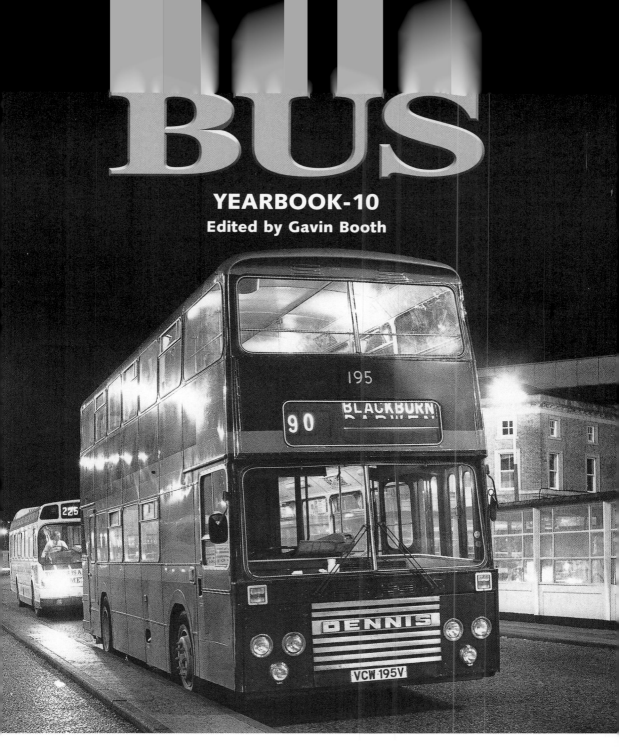

Ian Allan
PUBLISHING

Contents

First published 2004

ISBN 0 7110 2996 2

All rights reserved. No part of this book may be reproduced or transmitted in any form or
by any means, electronic or mechanical, including photocopying, recording or by and
information storage and retrieval system, without permission from the Publisher in writing.

© Ian Allan Publishing Ltd 2004

Design by Hieroglyph

Published by Ian Allan Publishing

An imprint of Ian Allan Publishing Ltd, Hersham, Surrey KT12 4RG

Printed by Ian Allan Printing Ltd, Hersham, Surrey KT12 4RG

Code: 0403/B1

Introduction

I ALWAYS HOPE READERS GET AS MUCH enjoyment when they read the latest *Classic Bus Yearbook* as I do when the contributors submit the articles to me. The wide range of interests and periods covered in the book reflect the readership of the bi-monthly *Classic Bus* magazine, which uses the strapline 'Remembering buses the way they used to be'. There has been some debate in the magazine's pages about what era we should be covering, with some readers arguing passionately that interest in buses really stopped with the last halfcab double-decker. Needless to say, there are other readers whose first memories are firmly rooted in the era of rear-engined buses, Bus Grants, PTEs, NBC corporate liveries and the like, and we try to cater for them too.

So it is with the tenth CB Yearbook. We have articles that deal with the products of one of the short-lived postwar coachbuilders, Barnards, by Geoff Burrows, and the 1930s production of one of the most famous coachbuilding names, Weymann, by Alan Townsin. We also look at the fashion for forward entrance front-engine double-deckers from the 1930s through to the 1960s, described by David Wayman.

Two of the most popular bus companies are covered in articles about the last days of Southdown as many wish to remember it, by Michael Baker, and an episode that many might prefer to forget, London Transport's flirtation with bus of the AEC Merlin and Swift families, by Mike Lloyd, who worked on them.

The changes to the bus operators serving Colchester over the past 50 years are covered in a Geoff Mills photo-feature, and the rush to rebody older chassis in the bus-starved years following World War 2 are recalled in a Michael Dryhurst feature looking particularly at the company-owned BET and Tilling group fleets. Some of the main events in Scotland 25 years ago are illustrated in a colour feature.

That master of night bus photography, John Robinson, shares some of his secrets and some of his fine night shots, and David Thrower describes Manchester's trolleybus system, which was introduced amid great controversy.

As always we include popular features from the bi-monthly magazine, *Classic Bus* – one of Larry Goddard's coloured photographs that have proved popular with readers, a Classic Wonderbus and four Checkpoint features from Alan Millar, and one of Roger Davies's characteristic 'Roger and out' pieces.

Gavin Booth
Edinburgh

Title page: John Robinson expected Hyndburn's dark blue/red livery to be difficult to photograph at night, but this March 1989 view of no.195, a Dennis Dominator/East Lancs, at Blackburn bus station, proves otherwise.

Front cover: John Robinson's night photography has become much admired, and in this book he describes how he started taking night photos and how he achieves these impressive results. John's cover photo shows the preserved 1975 Leicester City Transport Scania BR111DH/MCW Metropolitan, no.301, at its old home, Abbey Park Road garage.

Back cover: Another John Robinson shot, a daylight one this time, featuring the preserved Burnley Colne & Nelson no.10, a 1948 Leyland Tiger PS1/1 with Brush body, climbing out of Barley with Pendle Hill in the background.

FEDD not

DAVID WAYMAN describes how the forward entrance double-decker re-emerged phoenix-like after years in the wilderness. Additional material by Geoff Burrows

'THERE'S ONLY ONE PLACE FOR THE entrance on a double-decker, and that's at the back.' So said the chief engineer of Northern Coachbuilders in Newcastle upon Tyne more than half a century ago, and he ought to have known. He'd previously been chief designer at Loughborough-based Brush, which must have made him bristle with excitement. In late prewar years, Brush had produced some forward entrance double-deck bodies for the Birmingham & Midland Motor Omnibus Co – yes, the mighty Midland Red. Then during World War 2 and shortly after it, to the orders of the locally-based Northern General Transport Company and associates, his Tyneside firm had constructed new rear entrance

double-deck bodies on some prewar chassis that had originally been fitted with forward entrance double-deck bodywork built elsewhere. Buses with forward entrance double-deck bodywork had achieved limited but significant acceptance during the prewar era, but throughout the immediate postwar period the number placed in service amounted to no more than a tiny percentage of the national total. Unless otherwise stated, incidentally, 'double-decker' here means the type built from the late 1920s where the engine was over the front axle, which on such chassis was generally just about as far forward as it could be.

Until the late 1950s, other than for the few remaining exceptions, including some with centre

REDD

entrance and some with rear entrance and forward exit, double-deck bodies had one opening for passengers. This was at the nearside rear corner of the body and therefore behind the rear axle. In most cases it was without doors. But a forward entrance had to be behind the front axle, either immediately or almost so, and there were a few people in the bus-operating industry who were wishing that someone would hurry up and design the Guy Wulfrunian to show that there was another way of doing it. But no one achieved that until late 1959 and even then, regrettably, there were snags and the model didn't catch on in a big way.

Back in 1957, however, there we were thinking that forward and centre-entrance buses would be gone for good within a few years. Then we opened our *Buses Illustrated* in January 1958 and there it was: an article entitled 'Ribble Giants In Action', illustrated with a picture of a new Leyland Titan PD3. The fully-fronted body was built by Burlingham, and guess

what? It had a forward entrance with sliding door operated by the driver.

'Forward entrance? Ribble, have you gone mad?' we wondered. The prototype had been tried out a few months previously on urban and interurban services, and no fewer than a further 104 similar buses were to enter service with Ribble during 1957/8, with more later. We couldn't think of anyone other than those

Opposite above: Among the company operators specifying forward entrances for late prewar double-deck bodies, in this case built by Weymann, was Trent Motor Traction of Derby. Further rarity is given to this example in that it is one of a quantity of Daimler COG5 chassis, that make being relatively unusual among large company fleets at the time – indeed until the Fleetline model arrived in the 1960s. Trent also operated prewar AEC and BMMO chassis with similarly configured bodywork.
John Fozard

Opposite below: The Midland General Omnibus Co of Langley Mill acquired forward entrance Weymann-bodied double-deckers before World War 2, in this case on 1938 AEC Regent chassis as shown by no.181. It was one of ten new in 1938, following 25 the previous year. John Fozard

Right: In the late prewar and early postwar era, the distinctive Barton fleet, based at Chilwell, Notts, contained forward entrance Leyland Titans with lowbridge bodywork built by Duple, a concern more usually associated in peacetime with single-deck luxury coachwork. This 1948 advert features a PD1, and shows the short bay immediately aft of the front bulkhead, within which the staircase rose transversely.

This DUPLE 55 Passenger Double-decker Bus is mounted on a Leyland P.D.I. chassis, and is of the Low Bridge type. It is equipped with a complete Heating/Ventilating system and has Electric-Pneumatic Sliding Doors. We will gladly send specifications on request.

Duple Coachwork now available for many makes of RECON-DITIONED chassis.

See our Exhibits at Commercial Transport Exhibition, Oct. 1–9. STAND No. 49.

DUPLE MOTOR BODIES LTD., THE HYDE, HENDON, N.W.9.

stalwart independents Barton of Nottinghamshire and Birch Bros of north-west London who had placed in service postwar deckers with forward entrances. (Go on, someone tell us there were others!) Oh yes, there had been West Hartlepool Corporation and independent West Riding Automobile with handfuls of postwar centre entrance specimens, but forward? Was this an isolated aberration or the start of a new trend? If the latter, we were keen to see how far it would catch on.

New length

But why the sudden change? So far as Ribble was concerned, it may well have been to do with the fact that the Titans were PD3, that is, built to the then-new length of 30ft, sanctioned for double-deckers only in 1956. Their bodies had 72 seats, an increase of 11 on the most recent, rear entrance, 27ft deckers in the

fleet. Aha – so it must have been prompted by thoughts of lost revenue because the conductor might not be able to collect all the fares before dishonest passengers started to hop off! But with a forward entrance controlled by the driver, went the theory, the conductor was free to concentrate on fare-collecting without the time-consuming distraction of platform supervision. It was argued that partial supervision of the platform by the driver had been seen to work satisfactorily for many years with single-deckers, and could now be extended to double-deckers.

Not mentioned at the time, incidentally, was the legal point as to who precisely would be blameworthy in the case of injury to a passenger while boarding or alighting if the conductor were elsewhere on the bus. However, said the un-named *BI* reporter with more

Above: **Eastern Scottish liked the Gardner-engined Bristol Lodekka and when the FLF models came along, took quantities of the longer and longest types. One of the latter, with standard Eastern Coach Works body, is seen here heading out of Edinburgh, a Lothian Leyland Atlantean in pursuit.**
David Wayman

Left: **Massey Bros bodywork was built in Wigan and this example, on a Leyland Titan PD2 chassis, was new to the local municipal operator, passing to the Greater Manchester PTE in 1974.**
David Wayman

than a 'tad' of logic, these new giants would of course be used on the busiest services, where the strain on the driver would be at its highest. In other words, the driver already had enough to do. There was also criticism of the design of staircase, ascending in a semi-spiral rather steeply to the rear.

Nevertheless, forward entrance deckers did gain some degree of popularity, on chassis of 27ft length as well as 30ft, across all sectors of the operating industry. But what were the pros and cons of the design?

On the plus side, the driver could see the platform. Passengers were safe while the doors, whether sliding

The Park Royal-bodied AEC Renown would not be everyone's choice as the most handsome bus, but there were probably worse. Sunny Stockport is the setting for this one, which was new as no.129 in the North Western fleet. It is seen after passing to the then Selnec Cheshire bus company in 1973, a division of the area PTE.
John Fozard

or folding, were closed. But if the doors were left open, or if as on some prewar types there were no doors, there was the additional danger that a passenger falling while boarding or alighting from a moving bus could be crushed by the rear wheels. (The type that was potentially the most lethal of all in this respect, however, was that with doorless entrance at the extreme front, such as London Qs and RFs, particularly when in motion on left lock). Further on the minus side, passengers aboard rear entrance vehicles had become accustomed to a reasonably good forward view, which was now seriously impaired. There was often reduced luggage space, and with many types the conductor had nowhere to stand clear of passing feet. Power operation of doors brought additional costs.

Structural factors

There were negative factors structurally, too. The horizontal members are what give strength to a bus body, so, to cut a hole in the side reduces strength unless compensating features are introduced. Next, the vertical forces acting on the side are called moments, obtained by multiplying the distance from the fulcrum of the force to the load point, by the weight. Taking a

simplified look at that, it appears that a forward entrance body would be worse than a centre entrance one, but in fact the opposite is the case. This is because the first moment is from the front bulkhead to the entrance, and to this must be added another moment from there for the remaining length of the body. The weight of the central 'box' must also be added to the moment.

In the case of a double-deck body, the fulcrum point is at the front bulkhead. With a forward entrance body, a second bulkhead was normally put in behind the doorway, particularly with prewar and early postwar designs. This, combined with the staircase on the opposite side, would create a very strong 'box', and the

fulcrum for the rest of the body would be any point on the second bulkhead. The weakness of such a design lies in that is that there is no rear bulkhead. There is only the rear-end framing. This therefore needs to be very strong, as has the lower saloon floor to cope with the additional load. These factors tend to increase the total weight. Further strength is added by the intermediate floor. Unfortunately the big box at the front tends to collect moisture which of course is damaging at the best of times but in winter may also be salty. The worst of all combinations, however, is the design incorporating a short distance between the front bulkhead and the doorway opening, as on the Duple bodies for Barton on Leyland Titan PD1 chassis.

When the forward entrance concept was revived in the late 1950s, designers tended to forget that the 'box' at the front was essential to the maintaining of body strength. They therefore often omitted the second bulkhead or included one so small as to be merely a kicking panel for nearside front seat passengers. Some designs also incorporated a 'free-standing' staircase that made no contribution to body strength. The doors were power-operated and the only place for the mechanism was above the door. This meant cutting the remaining horizontal member, the cant rail, and even part of the intermediate floor. The sealing around this

area eventually failed, leading to corrosion caused by weather outside and the wet floor inside. (However, this also affected buses with front entrances as well as those being dealt with here.) Some manufacturers took these matters seriously and managed to eliminate many of the negative factors. Northern Counties was a case in point, their bodies on Southdown Leyland Titan PD3s being legendary.

Following Ribble's bold move, among the earliest UK operators taking delivery of forward entrance deckers were the Rhondda Transport Co with 20 Weymann-bodied AEC Regent Mark Vs; South Wales Transport with 26 similar; and the Ulster Transport Authority with 24 Leyland Titan PD3 bearing UTA-built bodies on MCW frames. In addition, three forward entrance 30ft deckers were exhibited at the

Above: **Alexander forward entrance bodywork is carried by this 1964 Leyland Titan PD3, seen carrying a substantial load on its home ground in the Scottish capital.**
John Fozard

Left: **This view inside a Roe-bodied Leyland Titan PD3 in the Oldham Corporation fleet shows something of the congested nature of the area between the platform steps and the staircase, with limited room for a standing conductor.**
J J Holmes

Above: **Northern General** was the only concern outside London to buy Routemasters, in its case Leyland-engined. Fifty were taken in 1964/5 and this example exhibits its forward entrance at Ferryhill en route from Newcastle upon Tyne.
John Fozard

Left: **Northern Counties** built this handsome body on this Daimler CVG6/30 in 1967 for the Swindon Corporation fleet. The bus is seen outside the depot of its present-day successor, Thamesdown, in this June 1982 view.
Geoff Burrows

1958 Commercial Motor Show, although this was the show at which the great talking-point was the introduction of the Leyland Atlantean in production form. The vehicles in question were a Park Royal-bodied AEC Regent Mark V for East Kent, a Northern Counties-bodied Daimler CVD6-30 for Potteries Motor Traction, a Willowbrook-bodied Dennis Loline for Walsall Corporation, and a Burlingham-bodied Guy Arab IV for Wolverhampton Corporation. At the same show, of course, London Transport's AEC-Park Royal Routemaster appeared. We all know the position of its entrance and that of more than 2,700 others that entered service over the following decade, excepting only the 'airport' RMs, one experimental specimen that was never operated in revenue-earning service with its original owners, and the Northern General 50. The London Passenger Transport Board had operated some prewar forward entrance double-deckers, however.

Death sentence

The Transport Act, 1968, virtually pronounced the death sentence on the conventional forward-engined double-decker of whatever body configuration, and so the final trend towards the type of bus in question covered only a little more than a decade. Many of the vehicles, however, lasted into the 1980s.

There were those operators who never followed the trend at all. One such undertaking was Manchester Corporation, which took some rear engine/front entrance buses in the early 1960s and then for a time reverted to the older combination of forward engine and rear entrance. Northampton Corporation, however, stuck to the traditional, well-tried concept to 27ft length virtually until this ceased to be an option in 1968. Some fleets contained a mixture of the following double-deck combinations: forward engine with rear entrance; forward engine with forward entrance; and rear engine with front entrance. In a few cases, operators such as Brighton Corporation and Southport Corporation adapted some of their forward entrance double-deckers for operation by driver only. This, however, was never a particularly sound arrangement either practically or ergonomically, particularly on urban services.

The operators mentioned in the in table (right) are mainland concerns that are included among those who acquired new forward entrance double-deck bodies on new or existing front-engined chassis from 1957. The number of vehicles in each case varied widely and some relatively large fleets had only a small proportion. Liverpool, for example, had only one; Alexander (Northern) had just two. No account is taken of operators who may have taken vehicles on demonstration or for experimental purposes only. Operators' names and the groupings are those obtaining when the vehicles were acquired, and no distinction is made between normal height and lowheight vehicles. **CB**

NEW FORWARD ENTRANCE DOUBLE-DECK DELIVERIES

LONDON

London Passenger Transport Board*; London Transport (and for BEA)

MUNICIPAL OPERATORS

Accrington; Ashton-under-Lyne; Barrow-in-Furness; Bolton; Bournemouth; Bradford (T); Brighton; Burnley, Colne & Nelson; Chester; Chesterfield; Darwen; Doncaster; Edinburgh; Glasgow; Great Yarmouth; Grimsby & Cleethorpes; Halifax; Haslingden; Huddersfield; Lancaster; Leeds; Leigh; Liverpool; Luton; Lytham St Annes; Middlesbrough; Nottingham; Oldham; Pontypridd; Preston; Reading (T); Ramsbottom^; Rawtenstall; Rotherham; Salford; Sheffield; South Shields*; Southend; Southport; Stalybridge, Hyde, Mossley & Dukinfield; Stockport; Stockton; Swindon; Walsall; Warrington; West Bridgford; Wigan; Wolverhampton.

BRITISH ELECTRIC TRACTION CO OPERATORS

Aldershot & District; BMMO* ('Midland Red'); City of Oxford; Devon General; East Kent; East Midland; East Yorkshire; Hebble; Maidstone & District*; North Western; Northern General**; Potteries; Rhondda**; Ribble; Scout; South Wales; Southdown; Stratford Blue; Sunderland District*; Trent**; Tynemouth & District*; Western Welsh**; Yorkshire Traction; Yorkshire Woollen District.

BRITISH TRANSPORT COMMISSION (later TRANSPORT HOLDING CO) OPERATORS

Alexander (Fife), Alexander (Midland, including Lawson), Alexander (Northern); Brighton, Hove & District; Bristol; Central SMT; Cheltenham & District; Crosville; Cumberland; Eastern Counties; Eastern National; Hants & Dorset; Lincolnshire; Mansfield District**; Midland General**; Notts & Derby; Scottish Omnibuses; Southern National; Southern Vectis; Thames Valley**; United Automobile; United Counties; United Welsh; West Yorkshire; Western National; Western SMT; Wilts & Dorset.

INDEPENDENT OPERATORS

A1 Service (Docherty; Duff; McKinnon; of Ayrshire); AA Motor Services (Dodds; Tumilty; Young; of Ayrshire); Bamber Bridge; Barton**# (Chilwell); Baxter (Airdrie); Birch Bros** (London); Blue Ensign (Doncaster); Bullock & Son* (Featherstone); Campion* (Riddington); Chieftain (Hamilton); County (Lepton); Hanson (Huddersfield); Harper Bros (Heath Hayes); Highland (Glenboig); King Alfred (Winchester); Lancashire United; Llynfi (Maesteg); Mayne* (Manchester); Liss & District/Creamline (Hants); Skill's (Nottingham); Smith (Barrhead); South Notts; Turner (Brown Edge); Weardale.

Key
* Prewar vehicles only
** Prewar vehicles also
# Early postwar vehicles also
(T) = Trolleybuses also
^ One source states that the final vehicle ordered by Ramsbottom was delivered new to the Selnec PTE.

Fourteen

No, not the odds against the disappearance of all but one of Colchester's bus and coach operators in the half-century since 1954 – they would surely have been longer – but, as GEOFF R MILLS describes, just one of 14 operators survived to 2004

FIFTY YEARS AGO THERE WERE THIRTEEN independent and one municipal psv operator serving the ancient borough of Colchester with stage carriage and express services. Of these, only Chambers of Bures has survived. The two major operators, Eastern Counties and Eastern National, still exist as fleetnames … just (after passing through Tilling, National Bus Company and privatised ownership into FirstGroup control) and the borough's buses are provided by Arriva.

Chambers was founded in 1877, motorised in 1919, and still provides the longest bus service in East Anglia: Colchester to Bury St Edmunds via Sudbury on an hourly frequency on Mondays to Saturdays. With well-presented modern vehicles and good publicity, the company seems to be in an excellent situation to continue well into the 21st century.

Five decades ago all the stage and express services were protected by the strict licensing regime introduced with the 1930 Road Traffic Act, and patronage was good and promoted healthy profit margins. In such a buoyant climate it seemed inconceivable that any bus or coach operator should wish to cease trading or sell out the business; even retirement was unthinkable. However, the Webber Bros (Empire's Best) had the audacity to do just that in 1960. Then in the same year the two sisters

owning both the Rowhedge village shop and the Fales bus service inherited from their mother, also sold out.

Taking 1960/1 as a yardstick, this was when the rot first set in with the long-established operations. The years had further significance to bus services in Colchester as the new bus station opened in Queen Street during February 1961, replacing the old St John's Street terminus, which dated back to 1926.

Blackwell's Motor Services, Earls Colne, Essex

Established in 1920, Blackwell's sold out to Hedingham Omnibuses in October 1965. Blackwell's operated the Colchester-Halstead via Earls Colne service, and its livery was maroon/cream. Fleet strength at the 'snapshot' 1960/1 period was 10 – a Dennis Lancet/Yeates, two Bedford SBs (one Yeates, one Thurgood), two AEC Regal IV (one Yeates, one Burlingham), and the rest Leylands: a TS7/Strachans, a PS2/Burlingham, two TD5/ECW double-deckers and this 1938 former Plymouth TD5 with 1954 Thurgood 39-seat body, photographed in May 1963.

Photos: Geoff R Mills

J D Best & Son, Great Bromley, Essex

This business was set up in March 1952 by the acquisition of C J W Sage. The business was then sold in February 1960 to R L G Catt and R C Swinn and then to F W Vine in April 1964; all were based at Great Bromley. The livery was cream/red and the fleet strength was seven – three Bedford OB (two Duple, one Plaxton), two AEC Regal III/Plaxton, Regal IV/Yeates, and this ex-Brighton Hove & District 1940 Bristol K5G/ECW 56-seater operated between October 1960 and October 1962 by Catt & Swinn. It is seen at Queen Street bus station, Colchester, in July 1961, still carrying references to the Shangri-La Caravan Park at St Osyth, who used it to convey campers to Clacton in 1960 before it passed into the Best fleet. The Best service ran from Colchester to Great Bromley via Crockleford.

George Digby, West Bergholt, Essex

The Digby business was established in May 1956 by the acquisition of V R Heath, West Bergholt. It sold out to Eastern National in November 1961. The Digby route was Colchester-West Bergholt via North railway station, and the fleet livery was cream/red. The fleet of five vehicles consisted of two Austin CXB/Plaxton, a Bedford OB/Wadham, an SB/Duple and this unusual 1951 Guy Otter, with Gardner 4LK engine and Longwell Green 29-seat bodywork, seen in St John's Street bus station, Colchester, in May 1959. New to Blake, Plymouth, it passed to Digby in 1958 from Witch Coaches, Warboys.

The existing users all transferred to the new site and were joined by Hooks, hitherto terminating in The Castle pub yard, and the express operators that had used bus stops in the High Street.

Later the same year G Digby, who had acquired the old-established Heaths bus service, sold out after only five years' operation. The following year the unbelievable happened when the Notices & Proceedings issued by the Traffic Commissioners at Cambridge confirmed the rumours that Moore Bros of Kelvedon was to sell out to Eastern National after nearly 150 years' service. Prior knowledge of the subsequent changes has helped to cushion the shocks but, coupled with the decline in passenger loadings, there will surely never be such a colourful variety of operators and rolling stock in the future, certainly in Colchester. **CB**

Fales Bus Service, Rowhedge, Essex

Mrs CG Mawdsley and Mrs G C Brown inherited the business, including the village shop, from their mother Mrs J A Fale, in January 1953. It had been established in November 1935 and sold out to Eastern National in September 1960. The livery was nut brown, revised to salmon pink, and the fleet strength was two – a Bedford OWB/Duple and this 1948 OB/Mulliner 31-seater, bought new. It is in the yard of The Plough pub at St Botolph's Corner, Colchester.

R W Hooks, Great Oakley, Essex

The Hooks business was first set up in September 1919 and ran services from Colchester to Great Oakley via Beaumont, Little Oakley via Horsley Cross, and Upper Dovercourt via Tendring Heath. The livery was two shades of green and the business was sold to Staines Crusader Coaches, Clacton-on-Sea, in May 1978. The six-strong fleet comprised two Bedford OB/Duple, two SB/Duple and two AEC Regal (one Thurgood, one Gurney Nutting). The two SBs are seen in Colchester bus station in September 1967. On the left is a 1955 SBG/Duple 38-seat coach and on the right a 1952 SB/Duple 33-seater that had come from Constable, Felixstowe.

Moore Bros (Kelvedon) Ltd, Kelvedon, Essex

First established in February 1815 and motorised in September 1912, Moore Bros was probably the best-known of the local independents until it sold out to Eastern National in February 1963. It ran services from Colchester to Braintree via Coggeshall, Chelmsford via Kelvedon and Witham, Tiptree via Birch, Tolleshunt Knights via Tiptree, and Earls Colne via Messing, Kelvedon and Coggeshall. Its fleet strength was 39 – three Bedford OB/Duple, two Commer Avenger III/Duple, an Avenger IV/Yeates – and the rest were Guys. There were four Arab II/Duple dual-purpose, six Arab II utility double-deckers, four Arab II/rebodied Strachans double-deckers, eight Arab III/Strachans coaches, two Arab III/Strachans double-deckers and nine Arab IV (four Massey, three Strachans, two Northern Counties). One of the Arab III/Duple single-deckers sets off from Queen Street bus station, Colchester, in July 1962, on a crew-operated run to Messing. It ran with Eastern National for a few months in 1963, following the acquisition of the business. In the lower picture is a 1945 Arab II with 1954 8ft-wide Strachans 56-seat lowbridge body. The chassis had been new to Birch Bros, London. It passed to Eastern National 1963 and was withdrawn in October 1966. It is seen in St John's Street bus station in May 1959.

W Norfolk & Sons, Nayland, Suffolk

Motorised in January 1915, Norfolk's was established in 1866. It ran services linking Colchester with Stoke by Nayland via Nayland, Sudbury via Nayland, Higham via Nayland, Nayland via Boxted, and Nayland via Little Horkesley. Painted two shades of green/cream, the fleet had 11 vehicles: a Leyland Cheetah/Alexander, a Leyland/Beadle rebuild, three Austin CX/Mann Egerton, four Bedford OB (two Duple, two Thurgood), a Dennis Lancet/Thurgood, and this ex-Birmingham 1939 Leyland Titan TD6c with 52-seat Leyland body, acquired in September 1954 and seen on its last day in service, 29 December 1962, at the top of North Hill, Colchester.

G W Osborne & Sons, Tollesbury, Essex

Another of the well-known names, Osborne's was established in July 1919 and sold out to Hedingham Omnibuses in February 1977. The livery was two shades of red/white and the fleet strength of 20 comprised eight of the independents' favourite Bedford OB/Duples, four AEC Reliance/Duple, two former London AEC Regent III RTs, a Regent III/Strachans, a Regent V/Park Royal, a Bridgemaster/Park Royal, a Daimler CVD6/Strachans double-decker, a CVD6/Willowbrook single-decker, and a Crossley SD42/7/Duple. The Osborne's services were Colchester-Tollesbury via Birch and via Layer-de-la-Haye, and Colchester to Layer-de-la-Haye via Berechurch. The Regent V with 59-seat Park Royal lowbridge body, new in 1957, is seen in September 1959 at St John's bus station alongside one of Digby's Austin CXB/Plaxtons. The Regent was sold in 1973 to PVS Contracts, Silver End, and used on contract services to Lesney Bros (Matchbox Toys) at Hackney, London.

0803

Blackwell's Motor Service

6d

Williamson, Printer, Ashton

George Ewer & Co Ltd (Grey-Green), Stamford Hill, London N16

Also trading as Fallowfield & Britten, Orange Luxury and Ardley's, the Ewer business was established in 1919. The company withdrew from the East Anglian Express workings in February 1985 and operation of tendered London bus routes started two years later. The company was renamed Arriva London North East when the Essex commuter coach operations ceased in September 1998. The snapshot fleet strength was 156 – 92 Bedford SB (41 Duple, 51 Harrington), 28 Leyland Tiger Cub/Harrington, 28 Leyland Royal Tiger/Harrington, two Leopard/Harrington, and six AEC Reliance (two Duple, two Harrington). This Duple Donington-bodied AEC Reliance was unique in the fleet and is seen brand-new in June 1962 at Queen Street bus station, Colchester, on a London (Kings Cross) express to Felixstowe and Ipswich. Grey-Green express services from Colchester ran to London (Kings Cross), Felixstowe via Ipswich, Dovercourt, and Walton-on-the-Naze via Clacton-on-Sea.

G L Sutton, Clacton-on-Sea, Essex

Sutton's was established in June 1922 and ceased operations in September 1979. The livery was red/cream and the fleet strength of 16 (all with Duple bodies) comprised a Bedford OB, an AEC Regal III, four Leyland PS1, four Leyland Royal Tiger, four AEC Reliances and two Maudslay Marathons including this one seen caught in July 1961 Saturday traffic at Stanway, just four miles from Colchester town centre, with a full load from London (Kings Cross). It was one of a pair of Marathon III bought new in 1949 and sold to Bickers, Coddenham, in 1961. Sutton's operated express services from Colchester to London (Kings Cross) and to Clacton-on-Sea via Jaywick.

L A Went, Boxted, Essex

The small business of Went's was established in May 1927 and sold out to Hedingham Omnibuses in July 1991. Went's operated Colchester-Boxted and Colchester-Langham via Boxted services using four Bedford OB/Duples. One is seen in March 1960 at St John's bus park, Colchester; new with Palmerston, Eastbourne, it was acquired in December 1949 and operated until January 1966.

Established in December 1924, the London bus operation was sold out to the City Motor Omnibus company, Peckham, in March 1928. The company restarted in coaching in July 1928 and finally ceased in July 1960 when its express service passed to C W Banfield Ltd, Peckham, London SE15. The Empire's Best livery was two-tone blue/white and the express services operated were Colchester to London (Waterloo) via Chelmsford and Epping, and Colchester to Clacton-on-Sea. The seven-strong fleet comprised three AEC Reliance/Duple and four Bedford SB/Duple. This was the newest of three Reliances with Duple Britannia 41-seat bodies when the business was sold to Banfield, though no vehicles were involved. New in 1959, it passed to Barton, Chilwell, in July 1960.

Colchester Corporation Transport

Established with trams in July 1904 and motorised from May 1928, Colchester's municipal bus company was sold to British Bus plc in November 1993, thence to the Cowie Group in August 1996 and to Arriva Passenger Services in October 1997. The snapshot fleet strength was 38: five Daimler CVD6/Roberts, five Bristol K6A (three Park Royal, two Duple), four all-Crossley DD42/7, and the rest of the fleet had Massey bodies, comprising one Crossley DD42/3, four AEC Regent II, three Regent III, 11 Regent V and five Leyland PD2/31. The services (routes 1, 1A, 2, 2A, 3, 4, 5, 5A, 6 and 7) all operated within the Colchester borough boundary. At Severalls hospital terminus in May 1963 is no.19, a 1957 Regent V/Massey 61-seater, a typical Colchester bus of the 1960s, which survived in the fleet until 1973. Behind is no.4, a 1949 Daimler CVD6/Roberts 56-seater, which was operated until 1968, and which is now preserved at the Lincolnshire Vintage Vehicle Society museum in Lincoln.

No.1:
South Shields Corporation Transport

Born: 30 March 1906
Died: 31 December 1969
Parents: The South Shields Tramways & Carriage Company and British Electric Traction.

Where do they come in?: The original tramway company (without '& Carriage' in its name) introduced horse-drawn cars between Pier Parade and Tyne Dock in August 1883, but gave up in April 1886, defeated by poor patronage. The new company started the following March and added a connecting horse bus service between the Market Place and Westoe. According to transport author David Holding, the new operator had secured more advantageous track rental terms with the corporation. BET was buying up tramways in the area and acquired the South Shields company in 1899. It wanted to live up to the 'E' word in its name and electrify, but so did the corporation and it substituted its own electric service from 30 March 1906.

What went wrong?: The corporation didn't like private enterprise running the town's public transport. Two attempts at joint operation with BET's Jarrow & District Electric Traction came unstuck after short bursts of cordial relations. BET ran a Jarrow-South Shields service over corporation tracks from 1908, with the corporation retaining revenue above an agreed threshold; it fell apart in 1911 when the corporation wanted a bigger share. Joint working of the same route began in 1922, but losses by the corporation ended this in 1927. However, the failure of the first service led to South Shields buying its first, far from ordinary buses.

What were they?: They were for a feeder service into the Jarrow tramway launched in July 1914, connecting Stanhope Road with Green Lane, Simonside.

Okay, okay, nice to know that, but what made them extraordinary?: They were Edison accumulator electric buses. A charging station at Stanhope Road provided them with power to make 18 round trips (45 miles) a day and they lasted until 1919, when petrol-engined buses took over and the Edisons were converted into motorbuses.

And the bus reigned supreme?: Not at all. The bus fleet remained in single figures throughout the 1920s and the 60-car tramway system continued to be developed, with a modern single-decker added in 1936. Abandonment didn't begin until 1938 and the final line, the 1922-built Moon Street-Ridgeway route over sleeper track to Cleadon, lasted until 1946. When South Shields did expand its bus operations, its first priority wasn't to replace trams.

Why not?: That was its second priority. The tram tracks needed to be replaced, but that could wait until services were provided to new edge-of-town housing estates. It was to these that the first four trolleybuses ran in October 1936, replacing motorbuses between the Market Place and Prince Edward Road. More Karrier trolleybuses replaced the Stanhope Road trams the following year and there were 58 trolleybuses and 33 diesels by 1949.

Why trolleybuses?: Three reasons. One was that this preserved the generating and power supply systems from the tramway. A second was a general move to avoid using imported oil and support the local coal mining industry. The third was that an electrical engineer of some note had been appointed general manager in 1934, when the decision to replace trams first came under consideration.

Who was he?: Eric R L Fitzpayne, an Edinburgh man who returned to his home city the following year and who introduced trolleybuses to Glasgow in 1949 (and withdrew them in 1967) during his period as that city's longest-serving transport manager. He argued that trolleybuses were best suited to the needs of South Shields. Ironically, it was a future Edinburgh manager who presided over their demise in April 1964.

And who was he?: Richard Bottrill, who ran the Portsmouth undertaking after leaving South Shields in 1969. Salt spray corrosion had put paid to the coastal route to Marsden Grotto in February 1958, but the coal mining argument kept the rest going until road development prompted a closure decision in February 1962. All of this happened before Richard Bottrill arrived at the beginning of 1964, so don't hold him up as the bogeyman. He, however, did recommend an accelerated scrapping programme and the final figure-of-eight route was withdrawn in a matter of weeks.

What about the motorbuses?: Most were Roe-bodied Daimlers and Guys. The first Daimlers (COG5 single-deckers) arrived in 1934 and the last (single-deck Fleetlines) arrived after Tyneside PTE took over in 1970.

A single-deck operator, then?: By no means. There were no single-deckers in 1964. It bought a few Crossley double-deckers in 1947/48, and otherwise took mainly Guy Arabs, then manual gearbox Daimler CSG6 and CCG6 'deckers until 1964. It moved on to double-deck Fleetlines, then took a batch of ECW-bodied Bristol RESLs before ordering the Marshall-bodied Fleetline SRGs.

Its favourite colours?: Trams and early buses were maroon and cream, but trolleybuses ushered in a radical change to blue and primrose, to make them look like Bradford's trolleys. The Crossleys were painted in Manchester streamline style and blue survived until the undertaking passed to the PTE and donned Newcastle's yellow and cream.

Alan Millar

South Shields transport committee members inspect the first postwar Crossley bus for South Shields before it entered service in February 1946. It is seen against the background of the William Wouldhave Memorial, celebrating the inventor of first self-righting lifeboat, built in 1833.
Geoff Burrows collection

Reading betv

No, not a tribute to the tramway system in a Berkshire town, but GAVIN BOOTH on the joys of the adverts in old magazines

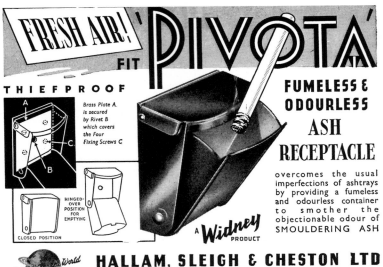

FRESH AIR! FIT 'PIVOTA'

THIEFPROOF

Brass Plate A. is secured by Rivet B which covers the Four Fixing Screws C

HINGED-OVER POSITION FOR EMPTYING

CLOSED POSITION

FUMELESS & ODOURLESS ASH RECEPTACLE

overcomes the usual imperfections of ashtrays by providing a fumeless and odourless container to smother the objectionable odour of SMOULDERING ASH

A *Widney* PRODUCT

Used all over the World

PATENT Nº 491775

HALLAM, SLEIGH & CHESTON LTD
WIDNEY WORKS · BAGOT ST · BIRMINGHAM·4

YOU KNOW HOW IT HAPPENS. YOU'RE LOOKING for something else – in this case Barnards advertising – and your eye is drawn to something equally interesting. I was looking for the Barnards ads – unsuccessfully – through early postwar issues of *Bus & Coach*, arguably the best of the bus industry monthlies, and I found myself smiling at the advertising styles, and in particular at the line drawings that had been produced to attract bus industry bosses to the advertiser's message.

Line drawings worked well because most ads were in black-and-white and the slightly dodgy postwar paper and some iffy halftone blocks meant that photos didn't always reproduce well.

Remember that this was in the late 1940s when advertising agencies employed graphic artists who worked at good old-fashioned drawing boards, with pen and Indian ink, without the benefit of instant lettering like Letraset, and long before desktop computers were available to generate instant 'art'.

There was presumably no shortage of work for these artists. One of the issues I looked at had 36 pages of editorial and – wait for it – 116 pages of adverts. Today's weeklies and monthlies would kill to have even half of that. In one of the issues I looked through, October 1949, there were 25 adverts for coachbuilders, which gives some idea of how hungry the market was

for new bodies, either on new or rebuilt chassis. Some of the names in that issue were the big ones that are still fondly remembered, like Metro-Cammell, Park Royal, Strachans, Willowbrook, and Yeates, but there were others that are distant memories, if they were ever memories at all: County Motors of Leigh, Crawford Prince-Johnson of Syston, Pearsons of Liverpool,

Before I pick out some of my favourite advertisements, what about the big names – what were their ads like? Remember, this was 1948-50, so although the big guns like AEC and Leyland were back in production after the war, they were being encouraged to concentrate on building up Britain's exports, much to the frustration of domestic customers, and so their ads often trumpeted their export successes. If photos of real buses were used in the ads, then the buses tended to be for overseas customers – AECs for Australia, Chile and Denmark; Albions for Hyderabad and the Transvaal; Bristol chassis for India and South Africa; Crossleys for the Netherlands; Leylands for Norway and South Africa; Park Royal bodies for Ceylon, Denmark, Greece and Eire. Daimler got round the lack of real buses to show with details of bearings, engine mountings and suspension. ECW featured prewar buses on the basis that its bodies were 'built to endure'; several of the others, like Foden and Strachans, resorted to fanciful artist's impressions of buses that were probably never actually built.

Then, as new buses filtered through to UK fleets, the photos start appearing: an AEC Regent III for Leeds, a Leyland Titan PD1 for Manchester, an MCW Regent III for Sheffield, an SMT Regent III for Duple, a Brighton BUT trolleybus. And when there was something really unusual and impressive, everybody jumped on the bandwagon. The September 1950 issue has no fewer than eight ads featuring the AEC Regal IV/Park Royal built for Hague Tramways; all are for suppliers of everything from fasteners and stainless steel tubes to rivets and safety glass.

More reasons for its economy..

The Fuel economy, which is now everywhere becoming associated with the Leyland 125 h.p. diesel, is to a large extent attributable to its patented governor. Stable idling and snap cut-off at maximum revs. are important features, but it is mainly because of its capability to govern progressively throughout the speed range, enabling steady road speeds to be maintained, that fuel bills are so comparatively small.

Leyland DIESEL BUSES AND LORRIES

LEYLAND MOTORS LIMITED · LEYLAND · LANCS

This new 67-passenger bus designed and built by Park Royal Vehicles Ltd., will soon make its appearance on the streets of the Hague. The body is mounted on an A.E.C. REGAL Mark IV chassis with an underfloor engine.

British-Built buses set a new standard of travel comfort in the Hague

Good for Park Royal Vehicles Ltd! This famous firm of coach-builders has been commissioned to supply a number of buses to the Hague Municipal Tramways Company. Good for the citizens of the Hague, too; for DUNLOPILLO seating will make travel smoother and more comfortable for passengers in these new British-built coaches.

DUNLOPILLO

DUNLOP RUBBER COMPANY LTD. (DUNLOPILLO DIVISION)
RICE LANE · WALTON · LIVERPOOL, 9
LONDON · 19-20 NEW BOND STREET · W.1
FOUNDERS OF THE LATEX FOAM INDUSTRY
SD/LT29

First over the border—

The ever-growing popularity of the trolleybus for civic transport has spread to Scotland. For the first services to operate in that country . . . by the Glasgow Corporation Transport Department . . . the obvious selection was B.U.T. Thirty-four B.U.T. 1641/T 3-axle models were ordered, and are now providing quiet, luxurious and efficient transport for the citizens of Glasgow. Civic and municipal authorities may be interested to know that B.U.T. has the only private testing ground in the country, over which ever vehicle is tried out under abnormally rigorous conditions before being passed for delivery . . . the "Best Under Test."

A·E·C LEYLAND TROLLEYBUSES

BRITISH UNITED TRACTION LTD.

HANOVER HOUSE, HANOVER SQUARE, LONDON, W.1

Telephone: MAYfair 8561/2

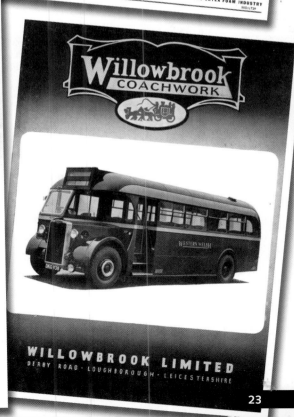

Willowbrook COACHWORK

WILLOWBROOK LIMITED

DERBY ROAD · LOUGHBOROUGH · LEICESTERSHIRE

23

A few examples of the ads that appeared in *Bus & Coach* at this stage illustrate this article – but back to the line drawings. Seating manufacturers were keen to advertise their wares with drawings. I particularly like the drawing in the ad for Lush seating (yes really) with a leggy lovely demonstrating just how comfortable the seats are. Or something. And there Carson seats, offering 'the individual comfort of an easy chair', with a splendidly middle-class couple reclining in an example of the company's craftsmanship. And another Carson seat abandons the picture of a real coach seat in favour of an armchair with a Dennis/Duple coach in the background.

G Beaton & Son Ltd, trading as Beatonson, allowed their artist to come up with a rather fanciful, if not unattractive coach to promote their 'coachwork accessories' *(right)*, though it doesn't actually say what these are. A later Beatonson ad identifies these on the front end of a coach, clearly Duple-bodied, mounted on something that looks like a cross between an AEC and a Maudslay.

CROSSLEY

FIRST CLASS TRANSPORT
FOR HOME OR ABROAD

BUSES · COACHES · TROLLEYBUSES · LORRIES

CROSSLEY MOTORS LTD · ERRWOOD PARK · STOCKPORT · ENG.
AND 50 PAGE STREET · WESTMINSTER · LONDON · S.W.1

WELCOME TO DENMARK

As the first of 3 of 10 "Regal" Mark III special 8 ft. wide buses ordered by the Danish State Railways was landed at Copenhagen, it received a salute from the King of Denmark's Yacht, the S.S. "Daneborg." A.E.C. buses are no strangers to Denmark, and these modern reliable and luxurious vehicles, each seating 44 passengers, will be warmly welcomed by the bus-riding public...

...they always are!

AEC SOUTHALL
PASSENGER TRANSPORT

BUILT TO ENDURE

10 Years old

In July and August 1937, six E.C.W. 56 seater "Long Life" double deck bodies were delivered to the MIDDLESBROUGH CORPORATION TRANSPORT DEPARTMENT. The General Manager of the Department now reports "Your "Long Life" bodies have fulfilled every promise made and look good for another ten years . . . they have definitely been trouble-free, and they are structurally perfect . . . they are not only good but look good and when repainted will look not only new but modern . . . . Congratulations on the design and workmanship."

These bodies have now done close on half a million miles including heavy War service, and, accident damage excepted, it has not been necessary to replace a single main constructional member during the life of any of the bodies.

EASTERN COACH WORKS
LIMITED
BUILDERS OF Long Life P.S.V. BODIES

HEAD OFFICE & MAIN WORKS: EASTERN WAY, LOWESTOFT
TELEPHONE LOWESTOFT 460   TELEGRAMS COACHWORKS LOWESTOFT

WINDOVERS LIMITED

BY APPOINTMENT TO HIS MAJESTY THE KING, COACHBUILDERS

COACHWORK SPECIALISTS
SINCE 1796

The "Huntingdon"
The Windover Body on A.E.C. Chassis which was awarded first prize in the International Coach Rally at Montreux in June.

THE HYDE, HENDON, LONDON. N.W.9
TELEPHONE COLINDALE 4031-2-3-4

Sorbo – 'the original sponge rubber' – uses a less realistic coach and a couple of men who look like MI5 agents exchanging secret coded messages boarding a London-Penzance coach. Another imaginary coach, a rather more realistic one albeit partly cutaway, adorns an advert for the makers of Tucker Hollow Rivets – better known as pop rivets.

And the product names were fun, in this more innocent age. Quickerstryp paint remover, Clepto seats, Plastahide upholstery covering, Pivota fumeless and odourless ash receptacle, Oddie Nuts for maximum fastening efficiency, Resistoid plastic covering, Homo number plates, and two firms using the Durex name, one making leathercloth, the other masking tape.

Off-bus products included the once-familiar Gledhill-Brook time recorders and Setright ticket registers. Intriguingly, that ad tells us that 'one clerk checks waybills for 6,000,000 passengers'; we just hope he was paid overtime. **CB**

Not so magical Merlins

Were London's AEC Merlins and Swifts bad buses, or just simply the wrong buses for the job? MIKE LLOYD had hands-on experience of them

London Country AEC Merlin MB95 at Windsor garage in September 1977, its front panel removed for towing, its rear engine access panels removed for repairs – a once-familiar sight.
J C Gillham

SEVERAL DECADES AGO, LONDON TRANSPORT bought from AEC a large fleet of vehicles which, after seeing service in the capital, were sold off to operators around the world. (Oh no, not another article about RTs or Routemasters, what is Gavin Booth thinking about?). These vehicles were widely regarded as a complete disaster, quickly acquired a very poor reputation, and many went directly to the breakers after relatively short lives in the London area. (Has Mike Lloyd finally lost his marbles? Surely he's thinking about the DMS which wasn't an AEC at all!). These were, of course, the rear-engined single-deck buses of the Swift and Merlin types which, like many other things of their era, the late 1960s and early 1970s, are best forgotten, but there were reasons for their existence and their lack of success and over 30 years on, their story is worth telling. My own experiences of the types are confined to those of the country area, later London Country Bus Services, the green buses. I know little about the red ones.

The story starts in 1965, a year that caused shock waves in London Transport for it was the first since 1958, the year of the great strike, in which the concern had failed to show a profit. One way out of this position was to reduce expenditure and to that end, it was clear that major savings in the wages bill could be made by abolishing conductors, but this solution was not readily available because one-man operation of double-deck vehicles was not legal, and single-deckers were not able to carry passenger loads equal to that of their bigger brethren. The British bus industry generally is pretty insular, but in an attempt to find an answer to this particular problem, cast a rare glance overseas. There, city services tended to be operated by long, one-man single-deckers, with two or more

entrance doors and lower floors than customary in the
UK, to speed passenger flow. To provide the carrying
capacity needed, such vehicles were often of the
standee variety, with minimal seating and a large area,
empty except for grab rails, into which many people
could be crammed.

This concept was not entirely new to Britain; for
example it had been tried by Moris Little in Edinburgh
in the 1950s without much success, although
admittedly with an underfloor-engined bus having the
normal three-step entrance. The people of these isles
preferred to travel sitting down and the standee
concept had few supporters, but maybe the time had
come to re-examine the position in the light of the
financial losses – a million pounds, in fact – being
incurred by LT.

There was another slight problem, too. No British
passenger vehicle manufacturer built a suitable piece
of hardware. However, on becoming aware of a
demand for such vehicles, the industry moved quickly;
the operators needed a vehicle 36ft long, the maximum
permissible, with a lower floor than usual, which
implied moving the engine from under the floor
amidships, and able to take bodywork with front and
centre doors; thus was born the first generation rear-
engined single-decker city bus in the UK. Of the major
manufacturers, Daimler produced its Roadliner
chassis, a much misunderstood and very advanced
vehicle which, had it arrived on the scene a few years
later, would have been, in my view, a great success. It
featured a gently sloping floor with the power unit
neatly tucked away under the rear seats, but to
minimise engine intrusion Daimler selected a
physically compact Cummins engine, unfamiliar to

British operators, and whose unique fuel injection
system, owing nothing at all to Messrs Simms or CAV,
was regarded with suspicion and ignorance. A great
pity, for this doomed the Roadliner to failure almost
from the start. Bristol, in direct contrast, got it
absolutely spot-on first time with the splendid RE,
which went on to have a long and well-respected
career and is sadly missed in many fleets today.

Commonality

Of the biggest players in the field, Leyland and AEC
had combined forces – a merger if you were a fan of
the Lancashire undertaking, a takeover if you
happened to be a Southall man, for by their
terminology shall ye know them – and this had resulted
in increasing commonality of components in the two
ranges, something set to continue and visually most
noticeable in the goods vehicles, where after the
takeover (what a giveaway!) both firms' truck ranges,
and indeed Albions, too, were given the Ergomatic cab.

To meet the demand for the new type of bus,
Leyland designed a chassis frame, lower than usual at
the front but sharply upswept about two-thirds of the
way along, under which latter part were mounted the
engine and transmission. When this frame was built up
with components taken largely from the Leyland
Leopard, it became a Panther; correspondingly, when
fitted with AEC Reliance units, it was the Swift,

Seen on its first day in service in 1970 is London Country SM128, a Swift 4MP2R with Metro-Cammell bodywork. The SM class buses were ordered by London Transport but delivered after the formation of London Country.
Michael Dryhurst

although originally the 36ft-long AEC version, with AH691 engine, had been intended to be called the Merlin, a name picked up by LT and retained despite its being dropped by the builders.

London Transport purchased an experimental batch of Merlins and serendipitously had them bodied by Strachans, not exactly a regular supplier of bodies to LT. The new chassis frame had a major defect in that it lacked rigidity, and there is much evidence to suggest that Strachans was the first bodybuilder to overcome the problems this posed by designed suitable mountings and building sufficient strength into the body structure to ensure that any excessive chassis flexing had no detrimental effect on the bodywork. The small fleet of 15 experimental buses eventually entered service in 1966, mainly in the central bus area, following prolonged discussions with the trade unions. Whatever the results of the experiments may have been, they could hardly have begun to come through before LT rushed out to order a further 650 vehicles, but this time the body orders went to MCW. This turned out to be the start of their problems, because that firm was unable to match Strachans' skill in coping with the flexible chassis. The order was split between red and green buses, and there were various combinations of door position, seating and standee arrangements but eventually the country buses emerged as 33 dual door 45-seaters and 75 dual door standee vehicles, originally with only 25 seats in the rear section. These joined the solitary green Strachans example.

They were impressive buses when new, having a superficial family resemblance to the RF (which the prototype Strachans vehicles certainly did not), and the rather subdued roar of the AH691 engine tucked away at the rear gave an impression of power. The exterior was in the traditional Lincoln green but with yellow relief, and the buses sported polished wheel rings to the front and chromed half-shaft covers complete with AEC badges at the rear; they certainly looked the part and gave no visible sign of problems yet to come. Inside, they were modern without being brash; their interiors were clearly based on Routemaster colours, although some had the older design of RT seat moquette. The standee buses looked curiously unfinished. Later examples had blue seat moquette that looked rather out of place. The standee buses incorporated automatic fare collection (although there was also provision for paying the driver), something new and seemingly up-to-date. Closer inspection revealed top sliding windows rather than the traditional LT winding drop lights and the flashing indicators were of a new style, no longer the so-called ears familiar on the earlier classes. LT took the opportunity to introduce the new buses to the public whenever they were to be used to replace traditional two-man vehicles by stationing one in a prominent position in the relevant towns and having staff on hand to explain everything. This seemed another mistake. Once the public had seen that their new buses were to

be chronically short of seating they immediately took against them, and the sobriquet 'cattle truck' was almost universally applied, something taken up in many cases by the local press. Eventually, in response to streams of complaints, a limited amount of additional seating was installed in the standing area.

Innovative ideas

LT had packed the new buses with innovative ideas. Apart from the fare collection equipment, there was the heating system which incorporated sensors and motorised flaps intended to provide fully-automated heating or a supply of clean fresh air according to the sensors' ideas of what was needed. In theory the system was a forerunner of the more sophisticated version to be employed on the Leyland National (see *Classic Bus* 64), although in this case with conventional floor-mounted heaters blowing air through ducts. The technology was not up to the job on the National, and certainly not on the Merlins, many of which managed to be freezing cold in the winter and to boil madly in warmer weather.

The automatic fare collection equipment fitted to the standee buses (MBS – Merlin Bus Standee) was a similar case of the technology not being up to the job, and while the machines undoubtedly worked perfectly in the showrooms of their makers, once they were mounted in a bus, and that bus was running along roads whose maintenance can best be described as indifferent, reliability disappeared in direct proportion to the jolting and vibration inflicted on the equipment. Change-giving machines declined to pay out, the various coin accepting devices jammed or failed to give tickets, the whole thing was a mess, and eventually

London Country MB94, an ex-London Transport AEC Merlin 4P2R with Metro-Cammell body, in Bridge Street, Walton-on-Thames, on the 463 route, formerly operated by RLH type lowbridge AEC Regents.
Michael Dryhurst

everyone had to queue up to pay the driver, exactly what LT had hoped to avoid.

The buses had a curious nodding gait as they made their way along the road, the standee versions being the worst as not only the engine and transmission, but all the seated passengers, were at the rear, mostly behind the rear axle, and anyone who has studied elementary physics will realise that the effect of this was to try to lift the front end off the road. The seated version, the MB (Merlin Bus) was certainly a better vehicle in this respect, the more even weight distribution helping.

Puzzle

Mechanically, the buses were perhaps a puzzle to the knowledgeable observer. Back in 1960, LT had experimented with three semi-automatic Reliances, the RW class, and amongst the results of these experiments were a problem with the engine, flywheel and gearbox on these vehicles being built as a close-coupled unit which led to overheating and premature failure of the flywheel glands; and there was a realisation that centre exits were not ideal for driver-only operation because the driver's view of the exit was not adequate for him to be confident that disembarking passengers were clear of the bus before he started away. The Merlins incorporated exactly the same close-coupling of engine, flywheel and gearbox,

London Country received London Transport's MBS4 in 1973 in exchange for an MBS. It is seen at Guildford in November 1974. It is a Merlin with Strachans body, originally used in central London as a Red Arrow.
M W Lloyd collection

and had centre exits, and one can only wonder if LT had learned anything from the 1960 trials.

The bodies were also curious. Previous large batches of new buses for LT had been the Routemasters, very strongly yet lightly built in riveted aluminium, a design which was to stand the test of time superbly. The construction of the Merlins' bodies however reverted to steel channel with hardwood inserts and panels fixed by woodscrews, in fact the same as the RTs whose design dated from 1938. All-metal construction was not new by the time of the Merlins' debut and LT had experience of it stretching back to the RFs of 1951, yet these brand-new buses reverted to a weaker form of construction and that on a chassis known to be excessively flexible.

This flexing, as perhaps might have been anticipated, resulted in distortion and cracking of the bodies, particularly around the area of the centre doors, a weak area in any event. Rainwater then entered the body, got into the electrical door operating gear, and caused havoc. The distortion also caused the doors to jam, and when they were open, electrical safety interlocking prevented engagement of any gears so the bus could not be moved. But even a new bus could be rendered immobile from this cause, long before its body had become damaged. To solve the problem of the driver's inability to see the centre doors, LT installed more technology in the form of a photo-electric cell and a beam of light, arranged so that it lit up when the centre doors were opened to allow passengers to leave. Passengers obstructed the light beam as they passed, and interlocking prevented the driver from inadvertently closing the doors and trapping someone. Great idea, but on the standee buses, especially at busy times, you could rely on

someone to stand in the way of the cell and the driver would be unable to close the doors. Public address systems were fitted to these vehicles, another innovation, but pleas from the driver to 'Stand clear of the beam' would result in a lack of comprehension on the part of most offenders until some more enlightened soul, anxious to get on with the journey, would point out the problem.

All in all, these wonderful new buses, with their space-age technology, were not the unqualified success for which their owners had clearly hoped. Various schemes for strengthening the bodies were devised, one in particular involving fitting external plates at cantrail level to all pillars. Eventually the automatic ticketing and change-giving machinery had to be removed and discarded, and the light beam and photo-cell system was superseded by an arrangement of mirrors which managed to give the driver a clear if rather diminutive picture of what was going on in the centre of his bus.

Trouble

So much for the bodies, then, but what of the chassis? They too gave trouble, and a major worry was the tendency of these buses to overheat. The Leyland Panther version of the vehicle had a front-mounted radiator, but for some reason AEC eschewed this and fitted a Reliance unit sideways at the rear, alongside the power unit. An angle-drive device, belt-driven from

the crankshaft pulley at the rear of the engine, carried plastic fan blades to draw air through louvres in the offside panelling and provide an air flow. This angle drive, however, proved an Achilles heel and had a very short working life, as did the plastic blades. One hot afternoon on late shift I was given the job of replacing one of these things so the vehicle could be used on the afternoon schools and factory services. I completed the task, went round to the cab and pressed the starter, to be rewarded with a wild shriek from the rear. A quick glance showed the fan blades failing to rotate, so it was time to do the whole job again, this time against the clock, with yet another reconditioned angle drive. The

Top: **MBS4 was received from London Transport in exchange for MBS15, which had been the only Strachans-bodied Merlin delivered new to London Country, although it does not appear to have been used, to judge from this June 1977 view of it, still in LCBS livery on the left of this June 1977 view at Wombwell, alongside withdrawn LTE Merlins that are just nine years old.**
M W Lloyd collection

Above: **London Country Swift SM464 in Dartford on the 499 route in August 1978.**
Geoff Rixon

London Transport's fleet of Merlins and Swifts greatly outnumbered the London Country examples. SMS603, a Swift/Metro-Cammell, works route 241 past Stratford in July 1979.
Geoff Rixon

idea of having the radiator alongside the engine seemed destined to result in the cooling air being, in fact, warm. Once the engine got hot, several things happened. The driver was alerted by the ringing of a bell in the cab, and it was common to see an MBS running up the garage approach road with a load of passengers aboard, bell ringing merrily, alerting us on the engineering staff that yet another Merlin was getting hot and bothered. Another interesting effect was that coolant and, not infrequently, lubricant too would be discharged in the form of a fountain through the filler flaps at the back of the bus. Following motorists did not like this, and I still recall one poor soul turning up at Hemel Hempstead garage in what had been a new, white car but was now a new grey one and being a bit put out. We spent quite a time carefully removing the remains of the contents of an MBS sump from his pride and joy, but on the bright side I don't suppose it ever rusted as the oil got into all those nooks and crannies where cars rot. This was quite a job, because in those days we had only diesel fuel as a solvent and a mains-pressure water hose, portable pressure washers being in the future. More usual, fortunately, was for the buses to dump the oil all over the road, and at least we had bags of absorbent granules to deal with that difficulty. In extreme cases, the Merlins would set themselves alight but luckily that was not common.

Another problem was brake squeal, and in a town with a lot of hills and a lot of bus stops, our buses attracted numerous complaints about noise. Earlier LT vehicles had brakes on which individual shoes could be carefully adjusted to give even, maximum braking effort and when combined with anti-squeal bands on the brake drums, produced an efficient and usually silent brake. The Merlins lacked this useful facility and we were quite unable to do anything practical to cut down the ear-shattering racket, other than hose down the wheels of offending buses in the often-vain hope that cooling the brake would quieten it down.

Some of our headaches resulted from London Transport's confident knowledge that it knew better than the builders what the buses needed. LT disliked filtration, and when the Merlins arrived, complete with engine oil filters, they immediately ordered removal of these unnecessary frills, with a suitable modification to alter the flow of lubricant, something that undoubtedly contributed to short engine life. Fuel filtration for these buses was still by old-fashioned cloth filters from the RT era, indeed, a plan to use modern paper-element filters on RTs some years earlier had been quietly dropped for reasons never made clear. One item they could not remove was the AEC oil-bath air cleaner, but during my time at London Country, I could find no evidence that anyone had been given advice or instructions on the maintenance of these units. One day, two of us decided to dismantle and clean out the air filter on an MBS, and we found it blocked solid with dirt. Cleaning it was no joke, but we

The LT Merlins had relatively long lives on the flat fare Red Arrow network of routes linking mainline railway stations with the City and West End. MBA580, with Metro-Cammell body, is seen at Victoria on the 507 in August 1980.
Geoff Rixon

did it, and thereafter the engine was able to breathe much more freely, which made a big difference to the overheating problems; naturally as the chance arose we did the remainder of the fleet, but clearly no-one had told the mechanics to do this job.

Failure

Difficulties such as these did not endear the buses to the maintenance staff but one fairly regular failure was rather welcomed, and that was a jammed starter motor. This was reached by lifting a floor trap at the extreme rear, right in front of the bench seat for five running across the back of the bus. Given a hot summer's day, a busload of young ladies from Apsley Mills all in miniskirts and a jammed starter motor and an MBS suddenly became quite an attractive bus after all! But I digress, and in reality, all these things, and others such as the need for constant handbrake adjustment, the difficulties of electrical relays that were not sufficiently robust and caused all manner of curious defects, and the preference of drivers for other types, made these buses very hard work to keep on the road. Once the Nationals began to arrive, drivers would find any excuse to turn in an MBS for a National because, far from defect-free themselves, they were easier to handle and rode much better. The passengers did not complain so much about them either.

London Country had inherited the green Merlins when they were but a couple of years old, but they already had a history of unreliability and unpopularity, and the lack of a Central Works meant that much-needed engineering support was reduced. LT's Aldenham works was used for some time, but its costs

escalated and the company eventually established its own works at Crawley. This place never seemed to get the hang of AEC engines, and right through the days of the Green Line Reliance coaches, overhauled AEC units were something of a gamble, premature failures being common. London Country persevered with the Merlins, but on top of all their other problems they were at 36ft long, too big for many routes. They staggered on until in 1978, when at barely ten years old, they began to be withdrawn and sold, many going straight to the breakers but some finding further use in Northern Ireland, while others worked for a while as airside buses, catering vehicles or other non-psv uses. Unwanted and unloved at London Country, they were, anecdotal evidence suggests, quite popular in the emerald isle, but several of our drivers expressed the fervent hope that they would quickly be blown to smithereens in the troubles there.

At this stage in their lives the Merlins suddenly blossomed, and made me believe that they were not really bad buses at all, they were simply being used for the wrong job.

Let me explain. Hemel Hempstead's Merlins, along with many others which were to be shipped to Ireland, were first taken to Grays garage in Essex, the nearest

to Tilbury, from which port they were to set sail. Engineering staff were responsible for transferring the buses, and a fixed-rate payment was made for each transfer. It was therefore in the individual's interests to get to Grays and home again as quickly as possible, thus being at home and at leisure while still being paid – silly, but we liked to beat the system. This meant that each vehicle was driven flat out all the way, as far as traffic conditions would allow in those pre-M25 days.

Top: **In St Albans in March 1977, London Country Merlin MBS292 on route S3.**
Geoff Rixon

Above: **Swift SM109 on route 418 at Leatherhead garage in the early 1970s.**
Geoff Rixon

On the 418 route at the Surbiton station stop at Claremont Road in July 1978, London Country Swift SM503.
Geoff Rixon

No account was taken by most of us of the need to look after the bus, it was sold anyway.

This sounded like a recipe for disaster, but in practice my various colleagues all reported, with degrees of surprise, that when the well-thrashed bus had arrived at Grays, far from boiling up or on the point of seizing solid, it would be purring contentedly, still full of oil and water. When my turn came, I too drove the vehicle quite hard, but not to its maximum performance (which, by the way, was nothing spectacular at all, the manufacturer's name 'Swift' being without doubt the least appropriate ever) because I dislike thrashing any vehicle unnecessarily. I found exactly the same thing, in fact, the vehicles even seemed to ride better for their long, fast run, and I am forced to the conclusion that they were actually intended as coaches and not as stop-start stage carriage vehicles at all. Maybe if we had had a batch with Plaxton coach bodies, improved engine compartment ventilation and proper maintenance, we would have been able to get good service from them on the Green Line routes. It's interesting to note that some of the red Merlins were exported to Australia, a place rather warmer than London, and they ran quite happily there once some ventilating grilles had been cut into the rear panels to improve airflow. This was something we often suggested in LCBS days, but staff suggestions were rarely welcomed or wanted, and no one listened. I was sorry to see the last ones go, but not that sorry. It was a sad finale to a long and formerly happy relationship between London Transport and AEC.

Shorter Swifts

There were, of course, also batches of shorter 33ft Swifts, the SM class with the smaller AH505 engine, the first few of which had Park Royal bodies. These shared some but not all of the problems of their bigger brethren. On the other hand, they had their own unique troubles and were little more successful. We had no experience of the shorter version at Hemel Hempstead until one, SM125, arrived for use as a trainer bus and I do not feel qualified to discuss them in detail; maybe that will be a chance for another author, another time.

The story really is one that can be summed up in the words, 'if only'. If only Strachans had bodied them all; if only there had been fewer innovative and untested ideas incorporated in one new type; if only they had been better maintained; if only they had all been fully-seated; if only we had been supplied with pressure washers to keep the running units cleaner and therefore cooler; if only the older brake design had been used; if only they had been used on express services – if all of these conditions had been met, perhaps they would really have been magical, and clocked up 20 years of good service. As it was, they barely managed half that, and only a tiny handful survived into preservation, a last few reminders of London Transport's massive misjudgment of the 1960s. **CB**

THE COLOUR OF MANCHESTER

In a popular series in the bi-monthly Classic Bus magazine, LARRY GODDARD uses his expertise to colour older black-and-white photos to capture some of the liveries used in the Manchester area

Full Metal Jacket

Oldham sits astride the highways running from south-east to north-west, connecting Manchester with principal Yorkshire towns of Huddersfield, Leeds, Halifax and Bradford, and north to south linking Rochdale and Ashton-under-Lyne. Cotton mills and engineering works, which had become well established in 19th century Oldham and the industrial suburbs of Chadderton, Hollinwood, Failsworth, Lees, Royton and Shaw, all demanded public transport for their workers.

I used to watch the teatime procession of workmen's buses labouring up Manchester Street and Yorkshire Street to the town centre on the 'magic' route number 1 to Waterhead, and noting the different bodies and position of destination panels on the old prewar buses was a regular occupation after school. My first conscious ride aboard one of the Leyland-bodied buses, fleet nos.102-4, came in 1952 while travelling home from Hollins secondary modern school. The school buses, which always carried route letter S denoting a short-working of the O and T route, were always veterans and they generally parked at Garden Suburbs until 4.00pm before drawing forward to 'our' bus stop. I pushed my way back down the queue in order to guarantee a ride on the bus of my choice, having noticed it was the third bus in the line up. The interior of the top deck looked bright but rather austere compared with products from Roe and English Electric.

Turning to this picture, the year is 1949 and Oldham Corporation is turning out its old-timers for the teatime rush hour. New buses have been arriving on the scene since 1946 but the corporation still needs to keep its prewar vehicles up to scratch to meet all-day service requirements. No.104 (BU 8575) is leaving Wallshaw Street garage following overhaul and a partial repaint, and the run to the Ferranti factory at Hollinwood will be a running-in turn. Delivered new in 1935, it is one of three Leyland TD4s with Leyland metal-framed six-bay bodies, and all would prove to be a good investment for the undertaking by outliving their contemporaries by a good margin. At time of withdrawal in 1954, they would be the last Oldham buses in the fleet with the pre-1935/6 route indicator layout. **CB**

Scotland 1979

What was happening north of the border 25 years ago?
GAVIN BOOTH offers a selection of photos

One of the newsworthy events of 1979 in Scotland was the acquisition in August by Western SMT of the two long-established Paisley area independents, Cunningham's of Paisley and Paton of Renfrew. On the last day of the Cunningham's operation, a former Ribble 1958 Leyland Titan PD3/Burlingham is seen in Renfrew, pursued by a May-delivered Leyland Fleetline FE30AGR with Northern Counties body from the Western fleet. None of the 18 Cunningham's buses involved in the acquisition was used by Western, but 10 Leyland Leopards from the 22 Paton vehicles acquired passed into the Western fleet.
Photos: Gavin Booth

With the take-over of Cunningham's and Paton, Graham's of Paisley became the last survivor of the legendary Paisley independents. At Graham's Hawkhead premises in August are three of the increasing number of single-deckers that joined the fleet in the 1970s. From the left they are S15, a Leyland Leopard PSU3E/4R with Duple Dominant bus body, bought new in 1978; S10, a Leopard PSU3A/2R with Alexander Y type body, bought from Rennie, Dunfermline, in 1976 – it had been a Leyland experimental chassis; and S14, a 1969 Leopard PSU3/3RT with Plaxton Derwent body, acquired from Pepper, Thurnscoe, in 1978.

Above: The Post Bus service network grew in Scotland in the 1970s, typically using Commer PB2000 minibuses with Rootes Maidstone 11-seat bodies, like this 1976 example, fleetnumber 5750072, seen on the Isle of Arran in April.

Below: A different style of small bus – a former Greater Manchester Transport 1972 Seddon Pennine IV.236 Midi working the City Rail Link service between Queen Street and Central railway stations for Greater Glasgow PTE. The orange livery was to create a link with the new Underground trains delivered that year in the same colours; a different orange (known as Strathclyde Red) would become standard for the PTE fleet in 1983.

Above: **The MCW Metrobus appeared for the first time in Scotland in 1979. MCW handed over the first two examples to Greater Glasgow PTE and Alexander (Midland) at SBG's Buchanan Bus Station in April. GGPTE's 'M42' is a 'pure' Metrobus; although it carries a number in the same sequence as the PTE's earlier MCW Metropolitans, it quickly became MB3 before entering service. Alongside is Alexander (Midland) MRM1, with this unusual style of lowheight Alexander body. Later Metrobuses for Midland had the more familiar RH type body, introduced the following year.**

Below: **Tayside Regional Council's buses carried this attractive livery of two shades of blue relieved by white. Although it had bought Volvo Ailsas and, less successfully, Bristol VRTs, since it was set up in 1975, in 1979 it bought a Dennis Dominator and an MCW Metrobus for evaluation purposes. Although more Dominators were bought, the Metrobus was short-lived in the fleet, and Ailsas continued to be favoured. The Metrobus, no.278, is seen at the Dock Street garage in September.**

Above: The Scottish Bus Group's Highland Omnibuses fleet wore this distinctive poppy red/peacock blue livery in the 1970s, and at Farraline Park bus station, Inverness, in June are D2, a 1970 Daimler Fleetline/Alexander acquired from Alexander (Fife) in 1977 and CD34, a Bedford VAM70/Willowbrook, delivered new in 1968.

Below: Yellow-painted Bristol Lodekkas were always fairly rare. This is Alexander (Northern) NRD3, a 1967 example that had been transferred from Alexander (Midland) in 1979; it was new to Eastern National and passed to Midland in the famous Lodekka/VRT exchanges. It is seen in Dundee depot in August.

Above: The Volvo Ailsa had been developed with the Scottish Bus Group in mind, and the group was a major customer. The first examples went to the Alexander (Fife) fleet, and Fife's first Ailsa, FRA1 of 1975 with Alexander body, is seen in May in the unfamiliar surroundings of Edinburgh's Holyrood Park, where it had strayed on a private hire. As it is a royal park, double-deckers are not allowed in it; a patrol van soon appeared to advise the driver of this.

Below: A previous breed of double-decker developed to suit SBG's requirements was the Albion Lowlander, and three of Alexander (Midland)'s 1964 examples are seen in Alloa depot in May. All have Alexander bodies, and the two buses on the right sport the traditional SBG destination display.

Above: The innovative Border Courier rural bus network was launched in 1979, supported by Borders Regional Council and the local health board. Buses provided links from rural areas into the Border towns, and also linked local surgeries and health centres with main hospitals in the Borders and Edinburgh. Eastern Scottish was the first operator of the Courier services, using five of these Bedford CFL with Reeve Burgess 13-seat bodies, featuring a rear compartment for medical supplies. ZC1 is seen at Selkirk in June.

Below: Apparently achieving the impossible for members of the Scottish Branch of The Omnibus Society on a May 1979 tour, Eastern Scottish ZB72 squeezes out of a tunnel beneath the Union Canal at Philpstoun, near Linlithgow. AEC Reliances like this were fast disappearing from the fleet at the time, and this 1964 example with Alexander Y type 49-seat body, was a particular favourite of Linlithgow's depot engineer, Harry Grant, seen at the wheel.

On other pages

Colour illustrations and photographs that relate to articles in the Yearbook

FEDD not REDD
Some operators moved on to forward entrance double-deckers but stuck to the traditional Leyland exposed radiator. This is Brighton Corporation no.31, a 1968 Titan PD3/4 with Metro-Cammell 69-seat body. Brighton had previously bought shorter-length forward entrance PD2s.
Gavin Booth

The Barnards story
The delightful cover of a 1948 Barnards catalogue, showing a Leyland Tiger PS1 with the company's service body.
Gavin Booth

The last days of the true Southdown
Above: **Leyland Leopard/Plaxton no.1177 of 1964 in the Ashdown Forest.**
Michael H C Baker

Lions and Tigers Below: **Fortunately, a small number of Leyland PLSC Lions survives in preservation to remind us of this ground-breaking model. Ribble no.295, a 1927 PLSC1 with replica Leyland body, is seen at Blackpool in 1995.**
Gavin Booth

Classic Wonderbus

Above: **Manchester Corporation was an early customer for the Leyland Atlantean, and before it moved on to the striking Mancunian body style, specified this design from Metro-Cammell. After it had passed to Selnec PTE, no.3806, a 1966 PDR1/2, is seen at Wythenshawe in August 1973.**
Gavin Booth

Left: **The Atlantean was also successful in export markets, perhaps most unexpectedly in the United States, where New York Metropolitan Transportation Authority ordered eight AN68A/2L with Manchester-style Park Royal bodywork. Four were in blue/cream, but the others, like this one at Leyland's test track in April 1976, were in red/white/blue to mark the US Bicentennial and the fact that they were Federally funded. After four years they were sold to Gray Line, and appeared in service in San Francisco.**
Gavin Booth

A shot in the dark

Above: **Parked at Carlisle bus station in January 1993, Stagecoach Cumberland no.705, a then-new Volvo B10M with Alexander PS type body, contrasting with no.752, a 1977 Leyland National acquired from Ribble in 1986.**

John Robinson

Below: **Standing at Lancaster bus station in January 1993, Lancaster City Transport no.308, a Leyland Leopard/Alexander Y type, prepares to operate an early morning journey to Abbeystead, a route formerly operated by Ribble. Also visible are two Stagecoach Ribble buses, a Leyland Tiger/Duple Laser and a Leyland National.**

John Robinson

Checkpoint –
Charles H Roe
Late-surviving
conventional Roe-
bodied double-deckers
included Darlington
Transport's 1964
Daimler CCG5s,
like no.4, seen in
June 1980.
Gavin Booth

Checkpoint –
Charles H Roe
Late-surviving
conventional Roe-
bodied double-deckers
included Darlington
Transport's 1964
Daimler CCG5s,
like no.4, seen in
June 1980.
Gavin Booth

Checkpoint –
The Midland Red
break-up
Operating for
Midland Fox in the
Midland Express
version of the NBC
'venetian blind' livery
in Leicester in
October 1984,
no.363, a 1974
Leyland Leopard
PSU3B/2R with
49-seat dual purpose
Marshall body.
Gavin Booth

The Barnards story

Son of Northern Coachbuilders? GEOFF BURROWS recounts the story of the Norwich coachbuilder, Barnards Ltd

TO THE CASUAL OBSERVER, there would not appear to be any connections between Northern Coachbuilders of Newcastle upon Tyne and Barnards of Norwich. That this was not so was discovered while the history of NCB was being researched.

An ironworks existed in Norwich from about 1826, and within a few years Barnards had established itself as one of the leading manufacturers of wrought ironwork. The architect and designer Thomas Jeckyll was commissioned to design a number of entrances to what are now called 'stately homes', and Barnards manufactured many of the handsome forged wrought iron gates and grilles for these. Included in these were those at the Bank of England, and the Norfolk Gates at the entrance to the Royal Park at Sandringham. Much of the company's work was more mundane, such as the fences required between the gates. Barnards in fact made quite a name for themselves with the manufacture of galvanised mesh wire netting, many miles of which were sent to Australia for rabbit fencing.

For a company based in a predominantly agricultural area, it was perhaps inevitable that it would also be involved in the manufacture of agricultural implements. These skills became refined into the production of every conceivable kind of truck and trailer for use on the field and farm. For this a large stock of well-seasoned timber was required, and may well have been one of the attractions that drew Horace Hatton and Jack Herdman to Barnards when they left Northern Coachbuilders Ltd in 1948. It is not known who made the first approaches, but almost immediately it became apparent that coachbuilding was to become one of the principal occupations at Barnards. Hatton had been chief engineer and latterly general manager of the Brush coachworks, before joining Northern Coachbuilders Ltd as chief engineer and designer in 1941. He was responsible for the standard NCB postwar double decker design produced in the years following

An attractive 37-seat dual-purpose body built on what the 1948 catalogue describes as 'special Guy chassis' for Butters of Childs Ercall.

Not what it seems. The artist's impression of the Barnards double-deck body that appeared in the 1948 catalogue. The registration number givers away the fact that it is a retouched photo of an Aberdeen Corporation Daimler CWD6 that had been supplied in 1946 with a Northern Coachbuilders body. The classic NCB front dome shape gives the game away.

that conflict. Herdman was appointed chief draughtsman during that period.

The magazine *Transport World* stated in July 1948: 'Here is a large well equipped sawmill, ample floorspace, with reserves of coachbuilding necessities, amazing stocks of timber including the hardwoods needed, and such encouragement to self help as a ferrous and non-ferrous foundry, well equipped machine shops and plating departments. We were impressed by the great potentialities for modern body building.'

Range

Barnards managing director, W Le Neve Bower, appointed H W Hatton as coachworks manager, and J H Herdman as chief designer, and before long a range of bodywork had been announced. This included coaches, and both single- and double-deck buses, which could be built on any of the chassis then available, large and small. These were all shown in a brochure issued in September 1948, and such had been the speed of introduction that this showed photographs of completed buses and coaches. It also showed various types of commercial vehicles,

agricultural trailers and work in progress in the factory.

Somewhat cheekily, there was also a doctored photograph of what was clearly an NCB battery electric van with the caption 'Now in the design and testing stage are a wide range of battery electric vehicles scheduled for quantity production in the New Year'. None was ever built.

The new Barnards designs emerged as attractive if traditional single-deck buses and coaches, available for both normal and forward control chassis such as Leyland PS1, Guy Vixen, Wolf and Arab, and Austin CX models. It was the double-deckers, however that revealed their true ancestry. They were, apart from a few details, remarkably similar to Northern Coachbuilders bodies, and judging from the customer list the sales effort was obviously directed at NCB customers. One of the first was shown at Earls Court in 1948, a Meadows-engined Guy Arab highbridge version for Clynog & Trevor in Wales.

The main difference was in the type of glazing used. When the NCB body was designed, steel window pans with rubber-mounted glass was seen as the most up-to-date technology. Since then flush panel glazing had been developed, first by ECW and later by other manufacturers, and it was making a serious impact on the coachbuilding industry. Briefly, all that was needed

was a flat panel with a suitable hole cut in it, and a rubber section was fitted to the aperture. The glass was then offered up to a second groove in the rubber section, and a rubber beading was then pressed into a third groove, this locked everything in place. The result was a flush-mounted window with all the corners radiused. To remove the glass it was only necessary to remove the beading first.

The effect of using this 'Fastfix' glazing subtly changed the appearance of the Barnards body from the NCB version, particularly since all the window corners were now radiused. Nearly all the other details remained the same; only the rear dome was redeveloped, using a formula from an American textbook on body design, albeit intended for car manufacture. The NCB dome had been drawn in the traditional way on wall-mounted cartridge paper with full-size sections of all three engineering 'views' superimposed on each other to achieve symmetry. The resulting shape was a series of smooth flowing curves from the flat surfaces of the sides and back to the rounded roof. Except in one position, that is. A 'bump' could be seen, when viewed from certain aspects, spoiling the perfection of the NCB dome. The result of the Barnards recalculation was a smooth curve seen from any direction.

The other principal change was of what was at the time the bodybuilders 'trade mark', the shape of the

upper deck rear window. The new shape was a simple rectangle, with radiused corners to accommodate the new glazing rubber.

Artist's impression

The Barnards catalogue showed an artist's impression of the proposed new double-decker. It was simply a retouched photograph of an NCB-bodied Daimler CWD6, and the artist had even forgotten to delete the registration plate on the radiator. This showed it to be Aberdeen no.59 (BRS 559) of 1946. The windows had been altered to show the new 'Fastflex' glazing, with radii on all corners, but the emergency exit window, which could be seen through the side windows, had not been altered from the classic NCB tapered side design!

The single-deck vehicles were straightforward in outline and so were suitable for use as either coaches or buses. They were well-proportioned and handsome without being overtly showy, and well in keeping with the ideas of the times. While not having the classic looks of Weymann or Duple for instance, they were well suited to their purpose and certainly not ugly or

embellished with doubtful ornamentation. There is no doubt that if NCB had been in a position to widen their range, any single-deckers would not have been unlike the Barnards vehicles.

The recognition features on the full-sized models were the half-canopied roof alongside the driver's cab, the forward-positioned sliding door and the half oval back window. The restrained side flashes usually started with a point at the front, then ran horizontally along the waist before swooping down to include the rear mudguards, though some ended in a Duple-style fork. Normal control (bonneted) versions had twin-leaf folding doors. The emergency doors were at the back on these versions, as opposed to the offside front on full-size vehicles.

Seating on the coaches was made by the company, though many customers chose to have it made by specialist firms like Tube Investments Ltd. There was a choice of sliding or half-drop windows, and a sliding roof could also be specified if required.

Construction of all Barnards' bodywork was of conventional composite construction, though the roof as designed for NCB on double-deckers continued to utilise Hatton's lightweight aluminium structure, Consequently the same drumming noises that plagued many NCB bodies were set up once the bus got going.

Municipal customers

The municipalities of Dundee, Bradford and South Shields, all former NCB customers, bought double-deck highbridge Barnards bodies. Dundee was their best customer, with ten Daimler CVD6s in 1949 (ATS 901-10), and nine AEC Regent MkIII in 1950

This Austin CXB was one of five with Barnards bodywork supplied to Guernsey Motors in 1948. It was retained on the island for many years, used for 'vintage' tours long after the remainder had been scrapped. This remarkable survivor was then sold to an operator on the Isles of Scilly, where it is seen here in the mid-1990s. It appears to have been changed little since it was built.
David Wayman

(AYJ 368-76), though Barnards advertisements in the trade press at the time stated that Dundee had 22 bodies on order. Bradford was the next best; it needed a small number of 7ft 6in-wide buses for the service between Bradford and Leeds. The local traffic commissioners were unwilling to allow 8ft buses on the route, as the Leeds end was served by trams that left little room on the roads for buses to pass. Barnards was only too happy to oblige with six CVD6s (FKY 574-9) in 1950, by which time most of the larger coachbuilders had standardised on 8ft-wide bodies. Although Bradford still had a large number of 7ft 6in-wide buses, no doubt civic pride required that the route be operated by brand-new buses if at all possible.

One Daimler CVD6 (CU 5091) in 1949 and two Guy Arabs in 1950 (CU 5226/7) constituted the orders for South Shields. Other double-deckers were supplied to Northern Roadways in Scotland and Rossie Motors, South Yorkshire. Lowbridge versions went to Green of Haverfordwest on Guy Arab chassis, Silcox (Pembroke Dock) had one (LDE 850) fitted to a Bristol K5G chassis, and a Leyland TD7 was rebodied for Birch Bros, the long-established and well-respected London operator whose roots (or should we say 'routes'?) went back to the early days of horsebus operation.

No trolleybus bodies were built by Barnards.

The bulk of Barnards' production went on to Guy normal control single-decker chassis. Amongst the many users were Bury Corporation with two on Guy Wolf chassis (EN 9180/1), Llandudno Urban District Council with three in 1948/9 (JC 8344, 9735/6), and one for Colwyn Bay (EUN 396). About 30 Guy Vixens were bodied, and a small fleet of five Austin CX buses went to Guernsey Motors, St Peterport. Following occupation by German troops between 1940 and 1945, the Channel Islands were given export status by the government, thus these vehicles qualified as 'exports'. One of these was kept on the island until fairly recently, and was used as an example of 'vintage' transport. It was eventually sold to an operator on the Scilly Isles, but its present fate is unknown.

None of the full-size single-deckers with Barnards bodies were bought by any of the very large operators, but several finished up in big fleets as a result of take-overs in later years. Barnards bodies were seen eventually in Potteries and BMMO liveries, for example. Bus, coach and dual-purpose versions were all manufactured. The list of customers included Bamber Bridge Motor Services, Stoke-on-Trent Motors and the Milton Bus Service, to give a few examples. Ralph's (Abertillery), part of the Red & White group, bought six AEC Regal III with 35-seat forward entrance bus bodies, JAX 109-14. These were amongst the last bodies built, in 1950.

Long-lived

Barnards bodywork was actually somewhat longer-lived than most of the contemporary NCB versions, due largely to the availability of fully-seasoned timber. There was, though, a feeling among a number of operators that some of the joints and panels 'worked' – that is, became loose, and that the structures were not as well built as those of NCB. This is interesting, because direct comparisons were possible in a number of cases. For example, the Barnards bodies at South Shields were rebuilt in the corporation workshops

during 1953, something that the NCB trolleybus bodies there never needed. Be that as it may, given the sort of maintenance that operators carried out in those days, any looseness in construction would have been addressed at the first overhaul.

Barnards traditional business of building farm equipment, including timber-constructed utility trailers, continued during this period. To this was added lorry cabs and bodywork, there being a number of skilled coachbuilders available to produce this work with the minimum of drawings.

It is a matter of surprise to find that Hatton repeated the error that he made at NCB, of not designing an 8ft-wide body. By the time that he went to Barnards, such width was becoming increasingly common and it was the stated intention of the operators' organisations to press the government for national approval of the greater width. In 1948 operators needed to apply for permission to use 8ft-wide buses on each road as required. It was a sign of their determination that most of them did this for every new route and many old ones too. One large operator, Manchester Corporation, had applied for and received blanket permission to use 8ft-wide vehicles on all except one of its routes. It should therefore have been seen at Barnards, as it was elsewhere, that the market for 7ft 6in-wide buses was already declining.

Stevenson's, Uttoxeter, no.8, a Leyland Tiger PS1 with 33-seat Barnards coach bodywork.

Guy Vixen chassis await bodying in the Barnards' Mousehold Works at Sprowston, Norwich. In the background are bus bodies on Guy Wolf for Bury Corporation and Llandudno UDC.

Hatton's other major error was to persevere with composite bodies when it was clearly time to change over to metal-framed construction. Supplies of good timber, properly seasoned, were rapidly declining. Many operators had suffered the misfortune of owning composite bodies that had been built with 'green' wood, and they were determined that they would never again buy such potential disasters.

As was inevitable, Barnards very small share of the coachbuilding market soon fell away, and by the end of 1950 no more was heard of that side of the business. The total number of bus and coach bodies built seems to be about 115, of which 37 were double-deckers.

Resilient

The original company was a little more resilient, it carried on with its previous work making fences and manufacturing components. In 1955, Barnards became part of Tinsley Wire Industries of Sheffield. In order to cut losses, production was transferred to Sheffield in 1990, and the Barnards Norwich works was finally closed down.

What then of Hatton and Herdman? John Herdman became the managing director of Bus Bodies (SA) in South Africa during the 1960s. The author has been unable to trace any further involvement in the industry by Horace Hatton, but it is unlikely that such a positive

Above: **Another luxury coach body, this time on Guy Arab III chassis, with the operator shown as 'Guy Tours', though the destination 'Oakengate' may provide a clue to its real owner.**

Opposite top: **An example of the Barnards single-deck body, on Leyland Tiger PS1 chassis, for Baxter of Hanley. The catalogue describes it as a 'dual purpose body of composite construction with "Fastflex" glazing and toughened glass throughout. Half canopy over cab with destination box and name sign. Near side front entrance fitted with sliding door and off side front emergency door. Fitted with Dapta type seats and interior parcel racks. Ample space for luggage in large boot at rear and attractive appearance make this vehicle ideally suited for private hire.'**

Left: **The last two double-deck Barnards bodies were mounted on Guy Arab chassis with preselector gearboxes for South Shields Corporation in July 1950. One of the pair, no.146, is seen here in May 1952 carrying Civil Defence publicity as part of a campaign to recruit volunteers. This bus was chosen because it was already suffering bodywork defects, and it was rebuilt in the transport department workshops at the end of the campaign.**

Geoff Burrows

and dynamic figure would altogether disappear. The firm of Bonds in Manchester began building new double-deck bodies about this time; they bore a similarity to Hatton's previous designs, though it may have been coincidental.

The other place where I have looked for evidence was the old-established firm of Mann Egerton, also of Norwich. The former NCB sales manager, Horace Beck (yes, another Horace) joined the sales staff there in 1949. It has not passed unnoticed that Mann Egerton built some double-deckers in the early 1950s for Sheffield and Newcastle, but it has not been possible to add any further information about these. There was also one built for Glasgow, which was shown at Earls Court in 1950. These were all supplied to former NCB customers.

So Barnards passed into history, and if it was not quite a 'son' of Northern Coachbuilders, then it was at least first cousin. **CB**

No.2: South Wales Transport

Born: Swansea, 10 February 1914

Parents: British Electric Traction and the Swansea Improvements & Tramway Company.

What was going on here?: The SIT had been around since 1874 and ran trams in the Swansea and Oystermouth areas. BET acquired the SIT in 1896 and took over a 999-year lease to operate the steam-hauled Swansea & Mumbles Railway, which to most outside observers was a tramway, electrified in 1929. These two companies ran feeder buses and BET set up SWT as a sister company to develop motorbus connections with suburban trams. Its first route, in May 1914, ran between Ynysforgan and Pontardawe and routes were established to Llanelly (as it was spelt then), Morriston, Port Talbot, Briton Ferry and Gorseinon. Acquisition of the business of F L Lewis (who became SWT's chief engineer) took the fleet up to 26 buses before World War 1 broke out that August.

Did SIT accept the situation sitting down?: Not exactly. It survived until 1953, although BET obtained powers to replace the Swansea tram system in 1936 and did the deed between March and June the following year when SIT-owned buses in SWT livery took over. This was a highly complex situation as the operator was obliged to share profits with Swansea council until 1957 and the council had a right of compulsory purchase after that.

Where did that leave the Mumbles tramway?: SWT took over the lease in 1927, but obtained Parliamentary powers to acquire the company in July 1959 and replaced trams with buses from January 1960.

The end of electric traction in its area?: Yes, but it made another important electric acquisition a few years earlier. In March 1952, it bought the Llanelly District Traction Company and its fleet of 26 trolleybuses and six motorbuses. Balfour Beatty, which generated electricity and – as a byproduct – ran trolleybuses and trams, owned the Llanelly company. The trolleys had replaced trams and passed to the South Wales Electricity Board when power supply was nationalised in 1948. While Balfour Beatty's East Midlands buses and trolleybuses passed subsequently to the British Transport Commission and BTC had a bus company in the area, the Llanelly system went to 100% privately-owned SWT.

Not even part state-owned?: Unusually not. While the main line railways bought into many of BET's regional bus companies in 1929/30, SWT remained a wholly owned subsidiary.

What happened to the Llanelly trolleybuses?: Motorbuses replaced them in November 1952. Some surplus trolleys went to Bradford. The company also had six Bruce-bodied AEC Regal III single-deck motorbuses, while some Regent III double-deckers were on order at the time of the takeover. They went direct to SWT, which replaced the green and cream Llanelly livery with its own allover red.

Why the Regal IIIs?: They were especially low, so they could negotiate low bridges in the dock area. In 1959 and 1963, they were replaced by eight Roe-bodied Regent V single-deckers – real rarities that were a mere 8ft 11in high with an inch to spare under the lowest part of the lowest bridge.

Any other acquisitions?: A notable series began in September 1962, when SWT absorbed J James & Sons, of Ammanford. James was one of several independents acquired by BET (in this case in 1950) in an apparent attempt to keep BTC off its patch. It ran only Leylands while SWT ran nothing but AECs at the time, and there were 13 Atlanteans including no.227, which was the first production example to enter service in 1958. The pace of change accelerated dramatically in January 1971.

What happened then?: The National Bus Company, which had taken over two years earlier, expanded SWT into a 540-vehicle fleet by absorbing around 180 buses in three smaller neighbouring fleets.

Who were they?: Two more operators bought by BET in the 1950s. Thomas Bros (Port Talbot) ran blue and cream buses, Neath & Cardiff Luxury Coaches the red and brown Cardiff-Swansea express coaches. The largest of the trio was United Welsh, established by Red & White in 1938 to amalgamate five businesses it owned in the area. BTC had acquired United Welsh with the rest of Red & White in 1950; it was all-Bristol by 1971.

Did everything settle down then?: No. Just one year later, Western Welsh's Haverfordwest, Newcastle Emlyn and New Quay depots were added, but only Haverfordwest remained after April 1972, when the other two passed on to Crosville. This took Western Welsh out of western Wales, but its name always owed more to a Great Western Railway shareholding than geography. These changes were symptoms of severe financial problems affecting NBC's bus operations in the area. To help ease its troubles, SWT sold some nearly new AEC Swifts to London Country and diverted an order for others in the same direction, the buses in question becoming the SMA-class Green Lines.

What happened later?: SWT's management bought the business in May 1987, with the new owners calling their holding company United Welsh and painting the fleet two-tone green; they sold out to Badgerline in February 1990. Today, the business trades as First Cymru.

Alan Millar

Five of these unusual Bedford YMQ/S midibuses with Lex Maxeta 37-seat bodies were delivered to South Wales Transport in 1982.

The last days of the true *Southdown*

MICHAEL H C BAKER
wallows in Sussex nostalgia

MY SISTER RATHER FOOLISHLY CHOSE TO get married on the day England won the World Cup in the summer of 1966. Of course my sister didn't actually know that England were going to reach the final when she had booked the church and the hall several months earlier but there it was, two dramatic events vying for the attention of a large proportion of the guests. I don't recall anyone actually sneaking out of the church to check on the score but certainly throughout the reception guests nipped out to the television in another

room and the cheers which erupted were not entirely on account of the best man's witticisms. The wedding took place in Hailsham, a pleasant Sussex market town beneath the South Downs whence my parents had retired a little earlier. And the location will, of course, give the clue to the subject of this piece. No, not weddings, but that glorious bus and coach company, perhaps the most popular there ever was, Southdown.

Hailsham had originally been on the main A22 Eastbourne to London road and had a coaching inn to prove it, but by the 1960s a dual-carriageway bypass kept through traffic out of the town – although not the Southdown London-bound coaches which plied the route and called in at the town 25 minutes after leaving Cavendish Place coach station, Eastbourne. But only long enough to pick up passengers who in my experience were a sober, respectable collection of citizens who wouldn't have dreamed of patronising a coaching inn. The vehicles used on the London run were a dream. I quite often drove up to London in my

Previous page: **Hailsham garage in 1968 with two of Southdown's legendary Queen Mary Leyland Titan PD3/Northern Counties, no.402 of 1964 and no.429 of 1965.**
Photos: Michael H C Baker

Right: **Michael Baker's 1948 Riley, with its potentially valuable registration number.**

Below: **Southdown no.26, a 1959 Commer Avenger IV with Burlingham body, awaiting disposal in Hailsham garage in 1970.**

Morris Oxford or Dad's Morris Minor and once, but never again, on a motor scooter. The scooter was a miserable experience, the Minor was all right, and just about the commonest vehicle on the road at that time, and the Oxford was perfectly acceptable, but the coach was heaven.

Sister Rosie's husband, John, had the good sense to be, if not an ardent bus spotter then at least interested in all forms of transport and had a penchant for owning interesting cars. In early 1969 I bought from him a 1948 Riley one-and-a-half litre for £70, which was what had he paid for it a year or so earlier. He spent the money on a 1936 Austin 7. The Riley was a lovely car, but not without its faults, the chief being a reluctance to stop. In those days I actually tinkered around with the inner workings of motor vehicles, not like now when you open the bonnet to find something like a spare warp drive from the Starship Enterprise. John and I tried every which way to improve the Riley's stopping power, to no avail. On its last journey I only got down the hill into Uckfield and avoided colliding with the 119 at the bottom by steering into the gutter and rubbing along the kerb. That frightened the life out of me; I never drove it again yet managed to sell it for £250 all on account of its registration, which was MUM 2. I used to collect my wife, Maeve, from her school in Catford – it had 2,100 inmates and teaching there was, as they say, quite an experience. The bottom end of each intake resembled nothing like anything her 22 years had prepared her for, but at the other end of the spectrum wonderful things were done. We went to see the drama department put on Hobson's Choice; one of the three Lancashire sisters was black with a strong Jamaican accent which you forgot all about five minutes into the play.

Personalised

Where was I? Oh yes, collecting Maeve from school. The cleaners used to look out of the window, see the Riley, and call 'Mum's here!' In the fairly short time we owned the Riley the personalised numberplate craze had begun, hence the large profit. We owned two more Rileys, both much more reliable but obtaining spares was a problem, so from time to time we'd resort to public transport. Getting back to Oxted where we lived from a weekend with my parents meant catching a 92 to Uckfield, almost invariably a Leopard with BUT-style bodywork, and a train from there. Once the Leopard had inched its way through the Sunday evening traffic jams that is.

Dad and I also boarded a Leopard one afternoon, a 191 jointly operated by Southdown and Maidstone & District, to Heathfield, in order to inspect a Ford Anglia. The Minor had failed its MoT on account of a rusting floor. Rather a pity, for it was in excellent condition in all other respects but floors were always a weakness of Minors – which didn't stop the garage that had failed it and which bought it off us for a song, rapidly getting it back on the road again. The Anglia was one of the early postwar, upright variety, rugged and basic but pretty indestructible, so Dad bought it, which pleased me if only because it had a CD registration, the same as about half the Southdown fleet. I borrowed it and took it on the ferry to Dun Laoghaire to visit Maeve the autumn of 1967 before we got married in 1968. She took one look at it and said 'Why are the wheels different colours?' It was a fair enough question but one which Dad and I had not considered, nor did we feel it detracted from the vehicle's positive attributes. Anyhow she consented to be driven to Belfast and back in it, even though we got a puncture in the Falls Road. Fortunately this was period when that troubled city was superficially at peace so the puncture was rapidly, if expensively, fixed.

Seen from Michael's parents' house in 1967, Southdown 1963 Leyland Leopard PSU3/1RT no.677 with Marshall bodywork on the Hailsham town service.

Best scenery

However we were actually discussing the joys of Southdown coach travel in the late 1960s. In the first place letting someone else do the driving – and in the summer of 1967 I'd just returned from driving an ex-RAF Bedford lorry from Gillingham, Kent to Katmandu, Nepal – was wonderfully relaxing. The journey, once clear of the London suburbs – we are now back on the Eastbourne, not the Katmandu, road – was through some of the best scenery south-east England had to offer. The climb through the North Downs by way of the Caterham bypass, which dated from the 1930s and was one of the earliest in the country, was the prelude to the rich farming country of the Surrey/Sussex border with Kent only a mile or so distant to the east, then once past East Grinstead and green London Transport RMLs on the 409, another climb took the A22 through the Ashdown Forest, a part of the world which will forever be associated with Christopher Robin and Winnie the Pooh. A A Milne lived here just off the main road whilst E H Shepherd, whose drawings did so much to bring the stories to life and who lived some 15 miles to the north at Limpsfield, spent many hours sketching amongst the trees, the clearings, and the streams where the first games of pooh sticks were played by the real Christopher who, truth to tell, was a rather lonely little boy. I knew an elderly lady who had been a friend of the Milnes.

Then it was over the trickle of water which was the infant River Medway and next a succession of pretty villages, all set deep in the woods which were the remains of the great forest which once covered the

Dusk at Uckfield bus station and Southdown Leyland PD2/12 no.808 with East Lancs body, new in 1957, prepares to set off for Lewes.

whole of Kent, Sussex and Surrey, followed with a stop at Uckfield where the Southdown garage adjoined the railway station with its level crossing at the bottom of the hill around which the town was set and which contributed to the magnificent traffic jams which stretched for miles on a sunny Sunday evening as visitors headed back from the coast. More attractive scenery followed, and at the end of the long straight stretch past the intriguingly named hamlet of Golden Cross and terminus, rather in the middle of nowhere, of the 16 from Brighton, swing off the A22 through the original, winding main road and so into Hailsham.

The vehicles Southdown put on the run were always up-to-date which usually meant Leyland PSU3 Leopards with Plaxton Panorama bodies. Four series went into service between 1964 and 1967 and with their restrained shades of green interiors and that wonderful bright green main external livery with a darker green skirt and the golden scrolled fleet name, they were the acme, as Roadrunner would say, of coach travel at its very best. Almost the best aspect of such a journey from London to Hailsham was that one was so much higher than in a car and therefore got a far better and more inclusive view of the passing countryside.

Plaxton was a newcomer as a supplier of coach bodies to Southdown, the 1964 batch of Leopards, nos.1175-9, being their first. It was a period when the Scarborough firm was outpacing all others in the UK.

Above:
Southdown no.802, a 1956 PD2/East Lancs, sets off from Brighton for Eastbourne in 1969, followed by a Brighton, Hove & District Bristol Lodekka FSF.

Left: **Guy Arab IV no.539 of 1956, with Park Royal 59-seat body, in Eastbourne garage ready to work the 192 to Hailsham and Uckfield.**

In 1968 Southdown Leyland Tiger Cub PSUC1/1 no.640, with Park Royal 40-seat body, sits in the sun after a summer shower at its terminus in Hailsham town centre.

Far older, and for ever associated with Southdown, was Harrington, whose works were only a short distance away from Southdown's at Portslade. Between 1961 and 1963, 54 L2T Leopards had been delivered, fitted with the supremely elegant Harrington Cavalier 28-seat body, numbered 1700-53. Being touring coaches they were not normally seen on the London to Eastbourne run, but often in the town itself on excursion duties. More likely to appear on scheduled services were the very last Harrington-bodied coaches ever to enter the Southdown fleet; these were 36ft-long Leopards with 41-seat Grenadier bodies, nos.1754-63, dating from 1964. Shortly afterwards Harringtons closed down, successful to the end but absorbed by Plaxtons and not seen as part of their future plans. Although Southdown had four more years before it would become part of the National Bus Company, and a little longer still before leaf green would start to replace apple green, the disappearance of Harringtons somehow seemed to be a precursor to Southdown's own demise.

Unpretentious

Hailsham had its own Southdown garage, rather a new one, a well-designed, unpretentious brick and reinforced concrete building dating from 1957, making it the last but one built by the company; Crawley's of 1959 was the very last. Conveniently situated in Mill Lane just up from the mill pond and my parents' house and close to where sister Rosemary had her wedding reception, it was home to some 15 buses. It always seemed to have plenty of spare room and in winter, as all over the Southdown network, delicensed coaches and some buses hibernated there. One in particular I remember was a Burlingham bodied Commer Avenger IV, no.26, dating from 1962.

Was there ever a more impressive rear – Kylie Minogue excepted – than the all-Leyland PD2 with platform doors? This is Maidstone & District DH396 at Tunbridge Wells.

To just about everyone's surprise Southdown developed a penchant for the curious Commer two-strokes, built in the old Tillings-Stevens factory in Maidstone. Until the early 1930s Southdown, like so many companies, had been a very good customer of Tillings-Stevens so it was a bit like coming home to buy buses once again from Maidstone. They were, however, very noisy and not really the no-expenses-spared, top-of-the-range type of product which was the Southdown hallmark. In particular the Burlingham bodies fitted to the Commer integral lightweights were nothing like as elegant as their superb Seagull predecessors, although the only time Seagulls might have been seen anywhere near Hailsham was if a Ribble or Standerwick example found itself on a South Coast tour, for Southdown never bought any.

On getting married sister Rosemary went to live in Uckfield and took up work in Lewes. This meant she regularly travelled on the 119/122 routes. The 119 was long enough, connecting Tunbridge Wells with Brighton, but the 122 laid claim to being the longest in the country regularly operated by double-deckers for its journey of four hours, six minutes took it all the way from the Thames at Gravesend to the Sussex coast at Brighton. If a Southdown coach was just about the tops in long-distance travel I used to think the company's halfcab Leyland Titan in its great variety of

manifestations – but each possessing that unique air of superiority peculiar to all that bore the apple green and pale cream livery – was its double-deck equal. The first Titans, TD1s, entered the Southdown fleet in 1929, the last halfcab varieties, PD2/12s with 59-seat East Lancs bodies, nos.805-12, 28 years later; it was these latter which often conveyed my sister to and from work. The first double deckers I ever saw with platform doors were the all-Leyland PD2s which Southdown and Maidstone & District both introduced on the 119/122 in 1951 and which my school friend Barry and I made an expedition to Tunbridge Wells to sample when brand new.

Endangered species

By the late 1960s the halfcab was an endangered species. Southdown had gone over to the full-fronted PD3 in 1958 and continued buying examples until 1967. These, of course, were the famous Queen Marys, so beloved of enthusiasts and popular with crews, of which many preserved examples (PD3s, not crews – though I can't be sure) can still be seen at rallies in former Southdown

Maidstone & District 1965 AEC Reliance/Weymann no.S53, south of Hailsham on the A22 on the 191 Eastbourne-Tunbridge Wells service.

territory and beyond. Heresy it may be, but I didn't initially take to the PD3, considering its Northern Counties full front far less elegant than the PD2s. To be blunt I thought it ponderous, positively obese. But familiarity and longevity have reconciled us, although not sufficiently to displace the PD2s from top spot.

One man operation – I don't think there were any women drivers at this stage – was rapidly spreading through the Southdown empire. There were fewer and fewer passengers on offer, particularly out in the countryside where they'd never been over-plentiful, all because of family cars like ours, I'm afraid, although of course we all got very cross on the odd occasions when we still needed the bus and it wasn't there any more.

One situation that did offer a lifeline to bus travel in the Hailsham area was the closure of its railway station in 1968. Part of a through route by way of Heathfield and Oxted to London, it was never electrified. The Hailsham to Polegate was the last bit to go, despite the inevitable local protests for it was well used, but once BR decided a line was going to close it seldom let logic get in its way. Consequently for a time the several bus routes linking Hailsham and Eastbourne did much improved business, to such an extent that a number of Titans, both PD2s and PD3s, as well as one or two of the last batch of Guy Arabs, were provided to serve as reliefs to the OMO Leopards which worked most services, during the periods of greatest demand. One evening my mother and I boarded an Arab at the bus station in Eastbourne (not to be confused with the combined garage and coach station just down the road in Cavendish Place) only to be turfed out as it wouldn't

start and we were transferred to a PD2. The PD2s belonged to the very last group in the Southdown fleet, the RUFs fitted with either Beadle or very similar East Lancs 59-seat bodies, dating from 1956/7. They were supremely handsome, although the slightly earlier all-Leyland Faringtons, by then all withdrawn, were my personal favourites. The Arabs, nos.524-59, had 57-seat Park Royal bodies, which were built to Southdown specifications and were virtually identical to those fitted to the final PD2s. Both PD2s and Arabs also worked the 199/122 until OPO took over, I don't ever recall seeing PD3s although I sure they must have worked some relief duties. As a race the PD3s were very much addicted to the seaside and throughout their lengthy careers with Southdown and its successors seldom seemed to venture on to routes which took them much north of the South Downs.

Oldest

So far we have looked only at Southdown, but Hailsham and Eastbourne were frontier territory. Then as now local services in Eastbourne were provided by the oldest municipal bus operator in the whole wide world. A number of the long-distance routes that headed into Kent were worked jointly by Southdown and Maidstone & District, which meant that the bus world was one of many colours. Maidstone & District was scarcely less popular with enthusiasts than

Above: **The original Southdown Queen Mary Leyland PD3, no.813 of 1957, at Eastbourne in 1971.**

Below: **Golden Cross, on the A22 road north of Hailsham, with Leopard/Weymann no.150 of 1966 and, in the distance, another Leopard about to return to Brighton on route 16.**

Southdown, not least because of its equally attractive livery of dark green and pale cream with silver roofs, lots of lighter green and black lining and, perhaps, the finest logo of all.

The 180 was one of the routes shared by Maidstone and Southdown. Very popular with gentlemen from across the Channel who were into property acquisition and development, it connected Hastings with Brighton by the inland route all long the ridgeway north of the Pevensey Marshes through Battle and such delightfully bucolic hamlets and villages as Woods Corner, Rushlake Green, Three Cups Corner, and Punnets Town, with Heathfield and Lewes. Another was the 15 which ran between Hastings and Eastbourne, cutting inland from Bexhill with its wonderful art deco De La Warr Pavilion, through Windmill Hill, Herstmonceux, another spot popular with Norman Conquerors as well as star gazers, Hailsham and Polegate. Although Maidstone & District bought lots of Leylands it was also very keen on Bristols and AECs, two makes that never graced the Southdown fleet. The very last AEC double-deckers M&D bought were 22 Mark V Regents with Park Royal bodies, which arrived in 1956. Eight of them were of lowbridge layout; the highbridge ones worked the 15 for many years so were a familiar sight in Hailsham. By the late 1960s they had been replaced by Reliance single-deckers with BET-style bodywork,

to be followed by many Leyland Panthers, Leopards and Daimler Fleetlines, all with similar bodies from a variety of makers. Weymann- and Marshall-bodied Reliances were a familiar sight on the jointly-operated Southdown routes along the Kent/Sussex border.

Which brings us to Eastbourne Corporation. I have a particular affection for the town for it was here where I met Maeve, in the Glastonbury Hotel on the seafront, to be precise, past which ran Corporation open-top PD1 Titans as well as various Southdown coaches. I was the hall porter and Maeve arrived one sunny (what else could it have been?) early June afternoon in 1967 with her mother from University College Dublin to work as a waitress (Maeve, that is, not her mother). I have written elsewhere of Mr Winkler, the very dignified Austrian manager who used to quite inadvertently terrify his guests with his somewhat exaggerated Viennese charm, so let us move on to the charms of Eastbourne's beautifully maintained, if not very large, fleet of blue, yellow and white buses.

Single-deckers

The most unusual were the only two single-deckers in the fleet. One was an East Lancs-bodied AEC MkIII Regal of 1950, no.11, the other, no.12, a Leyland Lion of 1935 with a Leyland body. This latter immediately

attracted my attention for a bus of this antiquity still in regular service in 1966 was something to be wondered at. It was the only survivor of five, the other four having gone to serve King and Country in World War 2, never to return. The Lion and the Regal lived, as befitting elderly Eastbourne citizens, a genteel, not over-stressful existence. I used to see them pottering around the town on the odd private hire job and such like and when they were retired in 1967 they both passed, in excellent condition, into preservation.

Leyland Titans and AEC Regents formed the bulk of the fleet. There had been some Crossleys, rare, but not unknown in southern England for Portsmouth and Maidstone corporations had bought some, but were now gone. Perhaps the most handsome of the Regents were the about to be withdrawn nos.20-4 of 1947 with that beautiful Weymann body which graced so many buses of the late prewar and early postwar eras. Eastbourne went on buying AECs, the last being four Regents Vs with East Lancs bodies in 1963. Titans continued to arrive for another four years, the very last being five, with E suffixes to their registration numbers, with bodies from, as usual, East Lancs. One of these was an open-topper. I can't say I thought them the most handsome of buses, although, as always, with their immaculate blue and yellow livery, and translucent roof panels, they were certainly distinctive.

Eastbourne no.56, a 1955 AEC Regent V/East Lancs, at Eastbourne Pier in 1977.

The St Helens-type front didn't sit too happily with the five-window, wind-down layout; the 1956 Regents were always my favourites of the 'tin fronts.'

The consequence of Eastbourne Corporation policies was that halfcabs were still being delivered when I became a semi-resident of the town – well an employee there anyway – long after Southdown had gone over to the full-fronted PD3 and Maidstone & District to the Atlantean and Fleetline. Traditionally white had been the predominant colour for Eastbourne open-toppers but at the end of the 1960s this began to be extended to other vehicles, with an acknowledgement of tradition in the form of a single blue band around the middle – perhaps a sop to the many blue-rinse moptop matrons who could be seen bobbing up and down on the lower decks.

One might have thought the most likely spot to find an Eastbourne open-topper was on the road to the celebrated cliff tops at Beachy Head. Not so. Although within the County Borough, Southdown had sneakily obtained the licence for this lucrative route in 1931 as successors to a firm called Chapman's who

Eastbourne coach station in July 1969 with two Southdown coaches, Commer Avenger IV/Harrington no.65 of 1962 and Leyland Leopard PSU3/3R no.1161 with Weymann Castilian body.

had originally provided a horse bus service. Southdown had worked this, the 97/197, with some unique six-wheel Tiger single deckers, rebuilt wartime Guy Arab open-toppers later taking over, being succeeded by the ubiquitous PD3s. Several batches of the PD3s had removable tops, easily distinguishable from their fixed brethren by their flatter roofs – when wearing them. Hailsham garage was home to several of them and during the summer when working as open-toppers they sometimes appeared as reliefs on inland routes, which could be a very jolly experience on a warm summer day.

Stunning views

One journey I would have liked to have made in an open-topper, but never saw one operating it, was on route 90. This ran from Hailsham westwards through the villages to Alfriston, one of the prettiest of them all and much favoured by tourists, then climbed up and over the Downs, with stunning views backwards towards the Weald and ahead across the English Channel, terminating in the resort of Seaford. Dad had a great friend with whom he had served throughout World War 1 who he used to visit in Seaford. He was a gardener who until his retirement had lived in Maresfield, a village on the A22 London to Eastbourne Road, and had the most delightful Sussex burr, an accent just about gone now. He went by the extraordinarily appropriate name of Herb Ashdown

and worked as a gardener for a large estate in – you've guessed it – the Ashdown Forest.

After visiting Herb we would continue, sometimes on the 12, which ran half-hourly along the coast between Eastbourne and Brighton, to Newhaven, a 12-minute ride, and there inspect the ships, one of Dad's loves. On a windy day the seas in Seaford Bay had to be seen to be believed. Hotel owners on Seaford front had the almost impossible task of keeping their hotels looking spick and span, such was the effect of salt on the paintwork, right up to the fourth or fifth floors. I've seen spray breaking right over the top of the lighthouse at the end of the long breakwater protecting Newhaven Harbour, and around this time there was an incident when a ferry only just made into harbour after battling enormous waves with a number of cars and lorries breaking loose and banging about below; must have been terrifying. Just as many Southdown coaches and buses retired to various garages for the winter, so Sealink used to lay up ferries at Newhaven and on one of our visits we came across the very last Southern Railway paddle steamer in the fleet, the former Southern Railway *Ryde* of 1937, perched high and dry on the mud, exposed by the falling tide.

Brand-new Southdown Bristol VRT no.501 in Haywards Heath in 1970.

This would have been 1970. The *Ryde* would not sail again and much that was familiar would disappear in the 1970s. The family would migrate westwards to Dorset, and Southdown, which had become part of the National Bus Company in 1968, would steadily lose virtually all its individuality. The Southern Region of the NBC took over its management on 1 April 1972; I had come across its first rear-engined double decker, a Bristol/ECW VRT, working a local service in Haywards Heath in 1970, and in 1973 the first Nationals appeared. Within weeks the lettering and NBC symbol would start peeling off some of those allocated to Eastbourne. Drab NBC green replaced the glorious traditional bus livery and coaches would be painted anaemic National Express white. The last halfcabs, the PD2s and the Arabs, went in 1971 although I came across a slightly earlier PD2 no.768, decked out in bright yellow training livery, in Eastbourne garage in 1974. Even later I found an ECW-bodied PS1, former coach no.1229 of 1947, serving as a luggage store at the back of Bognor garage

in the summer of 1973. Its longevity meant it lives on in preservation, as does one of the OCD PD2s.

It would be silly to pretend that the Southdown of the late 1960s could have been preserved in aspic. Perhaps the NBC was necessary. Certainly the growth of private motoring and cheap holidays abroad meant that the markets Southdown had relied on were fast declining. Eastbourne Corporation remains a major shareholder of the blue buses which have plied the streets of the town for 100 years; a remarkable number of former Maidstone & District and Southdown buses and coaches are still with us; and the Southdown Garage and its unique contents at Amberley Museum are unmatched in the preservation world. Nevertheless one can only regret that a company with such proud traditions is but a memory. **CB**

CLASSIC WONDERBUS

ALAN MILLAR's antidote to his long-running Blunderbus column in *Classic Bus* looks at the Leyland Atlantean

The decision to place the entrance ahead of the front axle on the Atlantean influenced the layout of British double-deckers for the past 40-plus years. This Liverpool Corporation example, with stylish Metro-Cammell body, demonstrates the front platform layout at Pier Head.
Gavin Booth

I READ SOMETHING THE OTHER DAY THAT said the only reason the Leyland Atlantean didn't become a music hall joke was because there were no music halls left by the time Britain's first rear-engined double-decker went into service in volume numbers. I feel I ought to acknowledge the comment – written rather nearer the times when these buses were far from trouble-free – before setting out to justify why this vehicle deserves to be considered as a Classic Wonderbus.

Yes, there were many problems with them in many places as operators used to buses with engines, drivers and gearboxes placed where nature – allegedly – intended got to grips with a layout more prone to overheating, abuse and other manifestations of a less innocent age. It also took time for the manufacturer to refine its initial clever idea into a more robust piece of machinery that ultimately came to be respected.

The music hall quip wasn't without a good deal of foundation, but in the end the Atlantean had the last laugh. And the fact that so many are still around as I write this in the first weeks of 2004 – a few handfuls still with their original owners – suggests that the model first put into production over 45 years ago had a lot more that was right with it than was judged to be wrong. Above all, it represents one of the few really big landmarks in British bus design. It changed operating practices and may well have played its part in maintaining a better bus service than might otherwise have been possible.

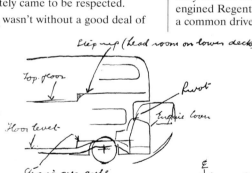

A Leyland designer's rough sketches show various elements of the Atlantean design in its development stages.

The clever part of the Atlantean story is that the manufacturer didn't allow itself to become too hung up on one part of the engineering. Leyland's world-class designers could simply have satisfied themselves by plonking an engine in the back of a Titan PD2 and

leaving it at that. Or they could have devoted their efforts to meeting the demand that apparently existed for an otherwise conventional lowheight double-decker. Both of these routes – the latter especially – probably looked a lot less risky back in 1952 when the first PDR1 prototype was being built, and we should be deeply grateful that men of vision took the project so much farther.

Just consider the fate of arch-rival AEC, whose innovation took it up what turned out to be a blind alley around the same time. Its prototype underfloor-engined Regent IV offered the potential advantage of a common driveline for double and single-deckers and in 30ft form could have carried even more seated passengers than an Atlantean, but it appeared to be a retrograde step as a rear-entrance bus with full-width 'halfcab'. When it appeared in 1956 (at the same time as the first Atlantean), the lowheight Bridgemaster was very much a 'me too' version of the Bristol Lodekka, an awkwardly laid-out conventional double-decker that only appealed to a small segment of the market.

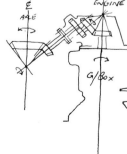

Just as AEC had been experimenting with side and underfloor engines from the 1930s, Leyland had been observing American and mainland European developments with rear engines. London's CR-class Cubs were its first attempts to put these ideas into

Nottingham had definite ideas about the design of its double-deckers, and Young's of Ayr, part of the AA co-operative, bought this Atlantean with eccentric Northern Counties bodywork to Nottingham style, in 1966.
Gavin Booth

practice and there might well have been a lot more progress had war not intervened. However, the outcome of the war might well have helped develop the Atlantean as a German national, an engineer by the name of Dr A Müller, led the research and development team behind the project.

The two PDR1 Lowloader prototypes – one built in 1952, the other in 1954 – tested the concept of a rear-engined double-decker within the operating parameters that most bus fleets understood. Although their engines were at the back and access to the driver's cab was through a door in the bulkhead into the lower saloon, they were otherwise conventional. The driver sat in what was more or less a halfcab and the passengers boarded and alighted through a rear platform. Okay, the engine was a more compact, turbocharged O.350 to squeeze into the space available and the staircase was routed around it, but it wasn't wildly different from a PD2.

A bonus was that it was a proper lowheight bus like the Lodekka. Sticking the engine in the back kept the cab low, fitting a drop centre rear axle kept the lower saloon gangway down towards ground level and the engine/gearbox position also kept the short propshaft out of harm's way in the offside.

That alone could have been about as big a turn-off as the Regent IV and Leyland deserves praise to the rafters and beyond for not building a 30ft version of this layout in 1956 when legislation permitted longer double-deckers. A lowheight, rear-engined PD3 wouldn't have been enough. Instead, the Lowloader gave way to the Atlantean, with the PD2's bigger O.600 engine and the chassis layout of a single-decker, with driver and entrance ahead of the front axle. Double-deck bus design had literally been turned back to front.

Courageous

It still was a lowheight and history shows Leyland took the correct courageous decision when it put the model into production two years later without that apparent competitive advantage. The 1956 prototypes were considered to be too sophisticated, noisy and expensive to succeed, so the manufacturer rationalised the design. It went for a separate chassis rather than integral construction and for a straight rather than drop centre rear axle.

Given the apparent demand for lowheight double-deckers, this might have looked like commercial suicide, but as I've already argued, lowheights were not in universal demand and several of the Lodekka's state-owned customers used their lowheights on routes served hitherto by highbridge buses. In any case, Leyland offered a semi-lowbridge version with five fewer than the standard 78 seats. This had a nearside sunken gangway towards the back of the top deck, which was far from perfect, but was a lot less awkward and clumsy than the offside sunken gangway along the whole length of front-engined lowbridge halfcabs of the day.

The point was that Leyland recognised there was far more potential in offering a 78-seat double-decker in which the driver could supervise boarding and alighting than there was in meeting limited demand for a lowheight vehicles. Especially as no other manufacturer offered anything remotely comparable, while the world, his wife and several of the in-laws seemed fixated by their chances with lowheights.

The 1958 Atlantean was 30% more expensive than the comparable PD3, but it had six more seats and the driver/passenger interaction was far more satisfactory. On the other hand, it was heavier, used more fuel, the cooling arrangements for a transverse rear engine were far more problematic than on a halfcab with a radiator facing into the wind, and there was lots of other unproven technology to get to know. The decision to buy was going to be a balance of pros and cons, but a bigger capacity bus was an attractive proposition 45 years ago.

With ridership falling and staff ever harder to recruit, many operators judged that the best way of containing these problems was to offer more seats less often and use big buses to provide a less frequent service. Many years after the revolutionary Leyland had gone out of production, I recall hearing this explained succinctly by Harry Blundred, the Devon General minibus magnate. Operators, he said, would look at how many passengers they were carrying, divide that by the biggest Atlantean they could find and arrive at the new frequency. That's what I mean about this bus changing the way the industry operated.

The big bus argument struck a chord with many potential buyers. The first four production buses entered service (in order, it is believed) with James of Ammanford (a BET company), Wallasey and Glasgow

Corporations and Maidstone & District and were followed pretty rapidly by a BET order for over 250 and a little later by major commitments from Newcastle, Liverpool and Glasgow. Birmingham City Transport took 10 and an ex-demonstrator in 1960/1, but no one should have been greatly surprised that it chose to place its bulk orders for Daimler's rival Fleetline, built in Coventry. And given the row that broke out when Coventry accepted a cheaper tender for the Atlantean in 1964, Birmingham made a wise political decision.

Weaknesses

There is plenty of evidence that those earliest Atlanteans came burdened with mechanical weaknesses. The very fact that a MkII version appeared in 1961/2 was evidence of some fundamental problems that had to be corrected. The original one-piece engine cover was replaced by a three-piece unit, welded gearbox mountings were replaced by more easily removed bolted ones, the centrifugal clutch was replaced by a smoother fluid flywheel, while the engine was uprated to 130hp.

Further evidence of Atlantean blues came with Ribble – which bought over 150 early models (several of them Gay Hostess and White Lady coaches) – reverted to the PD3 in 1963. Nor could any pricing incentive persuade the Scottish Bus Group to switch from PD3 to Atlantean, and a reluctant Leyland instead was dragged into developing the Albion Lowlander as a lowheight cousin of the PD3. In my own city of Glasgow, the corporation cut more and more square feet of wire mesh and extra ventilation into the engine covers of its growing Atlantean fleet as it wrestled with cooling problems experienced in many other fleets.

They didn't go down well with every driver, either. Some will tell you that the advent of the Atlantean changed their job for the worse. They were no longer protected from contact with their passengers and they didn't have the same intimate relationship with the engine and gearbox.

Eye-catching

These, however, were mere blips in the rise and rise of the Atlantean. A rise that had another revolutionary effect as key customers like Liverpool, Glasgow, Bolton and Coras Iompair Éireann – to name but four – took advantage of parallel developments in glassfibre and glass manufacturing to commission eye-catching bodywork for their Atlanteans. It was a move taken even farther when Bolton general manager Ralph Bennett moved to Manchester and helped develop the striking Mancunian design for his Atlanteans and Fleetlines delivered from 1968.

By then, the original perceived benefits of the Atlantean were being joined by another. One-person operation of double-deckers had been legalised from 1966 and a move to standee single-deckers was reversed in many areas as rear-engined double-deckers began to be operated without conductors. New Bus Grant came in from 1968, hastening the already inevitable demise of the last of the halfcabs. And for good measure, Leyland ended the 1960s with a monopoly of the double-deck market as consolidation of the motor manufacturing industry had brought Bristol and Daimler into the same fold.

It seemed that the Atlantean might have scored another triumph in 1965, when London Transport bought 50 – more or less to Stockton Corporation specification – for trials against eight Fleetlines and a still growing fleet of Routemasters. In one sense, this was a failure, as LT took badly against them, went on to order 2,646 Fleetlines and sold the Atlanteans to Hong Kong in 1972. But in another couple of senses, it was a good thing.

LT soon took against its Fleetlines in an even bigger way, but the problems with LT's Atlanteans helped prompt a major redesign of the model, leading to the launch of the revamped AN68 in 1972. Over 6,000 PDR1s had been produced over the previous 13 years and the AN68 total would top 10,000 in the 12 years that followed. New Bus Grant helped swell that total, but the performance of the bus cannot be understated. Sales to PTEs, municipals, National Bus Company, a few independents and some substantial export orders bear testimony to a design that enjoyed the endorsement of the industry.

It should have been ditched around 1978/9, when Leyland finally put its more advanced Titan into production. But that was a troubled project and orders from Merseyside and Greater Manchester PTEs kept the Atlantean going until European vehicle noise regulations meant that the model either was dropped or substantially re-engineered. It made sense to let it die then and for the already established Olympian to take its place.

The Atlantean enjoyed another period of glory after deregulation in 1986, when many operators suspended their fleet renewal and bought secondhand. Greater Manchester found itself with far more buses than it wanted in the brave competitive new world and big numbers of 10-year-old Atlanteans were among the modern tackle put up for sale. Newly privatised businesses soon realised that these bargains were a lot less expensive than hanging on to some newer leased vehicles – and they promised to last a good few years.

Most have now gone to the great bus depot at the end of the horizon, but the newest were built 20 years ago and most were kept at least for the full extent of their design lives. Readers of my Blunderbus articles in *Classic Bus* will recognise that success of that nature has been by no means guaranteed for every British bus. The Atlantean achieved that, remained a practical and economic tool for all of its life and changed the way that the industry operated. That sounds wonderful to me. **CB**

Lions and Tigers

JACK BARLOW recalls early encounters with animals from the Leyland zoo

Jack Barlow recalls his excitement when he first travelled on a Leyland Lion in Wallasey. This view of Wallasey no.1 was taken in 1926 before delivery to the Wirral town. A much later Wallasey no.1 would be a famous bus, one of the earliest Leyland Atlanteans in 1958.
Mike Sutcliffe collection

I REMEMBER, LONG AGO, BEING TAKEN TO the Zoo in Regents Park, London. We went by bus, which was very probably a General S type, but I remember the white board in the front lower deck window proclaiming 'To & From The Zoo'. Inside the park, one of the first places we visited was the Elephant House. Here I found myself, aged about six, being inspected by a huge dark grey animal. I was given a bun to give to Jumbo – I even remember his name! I very unwillingly attempted to pass the bun to Jumbo but, of course, dropped it on the floor of the cage. Jumbo, however, instead of taking it off the floor, blew it back to my side of the cage. This time, having got my courage back, I gave Jumbo the bun properly. It shows how intelligent elephants are.

Soon I found myself in another paddock confronted by a very ferocious-looking animal with a lot of hair around his head, large teeth and appearing to be definitely unfriendly, especially when he emitted a growl. He did not want any buns from children. He was a lion, king of the jungle. Soon after this came a paddock containing several very attractive and sleek-looking animals called tigers, famed for their speed. There were also some even speedier animals called leopards and cheetahs, names that all became familiar later in my life.

Enthralled

The story jumps forward a few years now, to 1926 in fact. By now I was enthralled by railways, tramcars and buses. Incidentally, the latter were often still called 'omnibuses', which was correct. Wallasey stop signs had 'buses stop here' on them. Mention of Wallasey reminds me of my excitement when the local newspaper had an item telling its readers that Wallasey Corporation had purchased five new buses called Lions and they were the most modern and efficient design yet produced and were on pneumatic tyres, a luxury indeed. They were seen in the town on driver training duties and on Good Friday 1926 they went into service and I travelled on my first Leyland Lion. The journey was from Harrison Drive to Seacombe on what became route 2 when numbers were later introduced. It was very exciting for me. Many of the

Above: **A 1927 Crosville Leyland Lion PLSC3 built for touring and private hire during the transitions from the charabanc to the coach, with features of both. The livery was grey with red lettering.**
Jack Barlow collection

Right: **Transferred from the LMS Road Motor Department when Crosville passed into railway control, this 1930 Albion Viking with Watson coach body has two doors, a folding roof, and, unusually, oil sidelamps, possibly reflecting railway views.**
Mike Sutcliffe collection

ordinary citizens of Wallasey also went on the new buses, just to enjoy them.

At the time most buses, whether municipal or company owned, were large and rather cumbersome. The new Lions somehow looked small and neat. It is hard to convey this to readers now who could easily wonder what all the fuss was about. Throughout the country the Lion won favour. The four-cylinder petrol engine proved very reliable and would always start on the coldest morning. Most were fitted with bus bodies but some coach bodies were fitted to Lions. Many survived, sometimes rebodied, until the late 1940s.

I remember a relatively long journey from Wallasey

to Manchester on an ordinary Lion bus. It was in 1927 and such was the good reputation already earned by the Leyland PLSC Lion that, within a year of its introduction, it was being chosen for special duties. I managed to be allowed to travel on this journey when Wallasey Corporation Health Committee wished to inspect new facilities just opened by Manchester Corporation. The members could have gone, as was usual at that time, by train from Liverpool but they decided that it would be much more pleasant if they went on one of the new buses. The one selected was almost new no.8 (HF 4535), a standard 31-seat all-Leyland service bus.

River crossing

The journey started with a river crossing. There were no Mersey Tunnels in those days and Wallasey Corporation catered for cross-river traffic with vehicle ferries called 'luggage boats', which ran in addition to the better-known passenger ferries. Buses were rarely seen on the luggage boats and no.8 found itself surrounded by the regular passengers, heavy horses that would be busy tossing their nosebags to secure the last crumbs of their feed. From Liverpool Pier Head we set off on what was then the only route to Manchester, the A57. It was a slow journey to start

with as we encountered many Liverpool tramcars of various kinds, all in their maroon and white livery. After the Old Swan there came some countryside (how different the scene is now) until Prescot, where Liverpool and St Helens tramcars met. From Prescot we passed Rainhill, crossing the famous skew bridge built by the Liverpool & Manchester Railway in 1829. Then came some miles of normal main road with curves and hedges. Warrington came next and this involved going through the middle of the town, of course. One street, Sankey Street, was particularly narrow and yet carried a heavy traffic both local and long-distance. We stopped here for refreshments.

The Cub was Leyland's small bus chassis and Crosville bought a substantial quantity in the 1930s. This 1935 example is a 1KP2 example with 20-seat Brush body.
Mike Sutcliffe collection

Some more country came next before Irlam and Eccles. Soon we reached the busy streets of Salford and finally for the last quarter of a mile we were in Manchester and drew up outside the main entrance of the imposing Town Hall. At once the bus attracted the keen attention of the local populace who obviously liked this modern vehicle in its unusual livery of light green and white. We were entertained to lunch in the Town Hall and were then joined on the bus by some local health officials to inspect the new baths and other facilities.

Later we returned to Wallasey by the same route, stopping for a meal at Rainhill. We reached Wallasey at about 9.00pm after what was for me a most exciting day. The councillors must have enjoyed it too because it led to similar trips being organised. It was really the start of what could be termed 'comfortable coaching', although this particular vehicle was certainly not a coach.

Rare Leopard

When passing through Liverpool there would have been a remote chance of seeing a very rare Leyland indeed, the Leopard model of 1926. Resembling a PLSC Lion in most respects, only two Leopards were built and both went to Liverpool Corporation, not usually a Leyland customer in those days. Although not seen on the Manchester trip, I did see one of the Leopards on another occasion. This would have been in 1928 when my father and I had gone to watch Everton playing a home match at Goodison Park. We travelled up from the city on a tramcar and as we alighted at the special football siding in Walton Lane one of the Leopards appeared, in service and carrying

passengers. To my regret I never travelled on one of these buses.

Long-distance services were getting into their stride by the late 1920s. Although there were no motorways and very few bypasses there were some quite long stretches of open road where a reasonable speed was possible. Leyland produced a chassis to suit these conditions with a six-cylinder engine, suitable gear ratios and a very smart radiator. This was named the Tiger and proved as successful as the Lion. It was purchased by coach operators in considerable quantity. About this time these long-distance vehicles came to be called coaches, whilst the vehicles on local routes were still buses. I remember a friend and I decided to try this method to come home from Uppingham School. The other boys thought we were mad. We had first of all to cover the 18 miles into Leicester and Midland Red provided the means in the shape of an SOS Q-type. We had a most exciting journey because the driver coasted down all the hills at a quite alarming speed. In Leicester we found the travel agent's office and waited. Along came a new Leyland Tiger, which took us to another office in Nottingham. We had about an hour here before another Tiger appeared with Manchester on the blind. This took us safely and comfortably to Manchester where we parted, my journey thence to Wallasey being

The lightweight Leyland Cheetah was popular with Ribble. This wartime view shows a 1936 delivery with Brush body.
Mike Sutcliffe collection

by train. The whole journey cost just over £1.00. Unfortunately I cannot remember the names of the operators. These early Tigers (the name lasted for years) certainly looked the part, were smart and comfortable and proved very reliable.

Longer-distance routes

The larger companies, many of them now owned by the railways, soon realised the advantages of longer-distance routes and either bought up the companies who had started the routes, or started their own services. Tigers were a very popular choice all over the country and I remember an occasion during a holiday in Tunbridge Wells in 1932, when we went to Dover for the day, travelling on a Maidstone & District Tiger. The hilly journey across Kent was completely different from the countryside that accompanied a journey on an Ortona Tiger from Peterborough to Cambridge, where a rise over a railway bridge was thought of as a hill! Nearer to home, several journeys were made on Crosville Tigers on the frequent Liverpool to Caernarfon service that took in the North Wales coast.

I will always remember a journey from Stranraer to Ayr on a Western SMT Tiger on a winter's evening in 1942. We left Stranraer at about 6.30pm and, with blackout precautions in force, the entire journey of about two hours duration was undertaken in complete darkness. We never seemed to be on a level or straight road but were forever going up or down hills or round innumerable comers, the sound of the engine and gearbox providing the only indications of the type of ground we were covering. It is in fact a most attractive scenic route but on that occasion remained all unseen by me. I had in fact just come from Northern Ireland

where I had been stationed in County Antrim and had been carried on many Lions and Tigers of the Northern Ireland Road Transport Board.

The next addition to the Leyland Zoo was not a baby Lion or a baby Tiger but just a Cub. It was a small and handy bus intended for minor routes and was really the predecessor of today's minibus. I remember journeys on the Island of Anglesey where, until the weight restrictions on the Menai Bridge were eased in 1944, Crosville Cubs ran all services.

The last addition to the prewar Zoo was the Cheetah. This was really like a 'lightweight Tiger', having six-cylinder petrol engines when built. I remember in particular travelling on the Ribble Cheetahs from Chorley and Leyland into Preston. They were smooth-running and nippy and much liked.

The between-the-wars Zoo was now complete. After 1946 the animals multiplied with a birth of Leopards, Lynxes and Tigers and even Royal Tigers and Tiger Cubs. I have to say that I enjoyed the early ones best. **CB**

Readers may like to know that the Leyland Society has recently carried out some research on the 1926 Liverpool Leopards and this was published in the quarterly magazine, 'Leyland Torque'.

CHECK POINT

No.3: Charles H Roe

Born: York, 22 May 1887
Died: 30 November 1965
What did 'H' stand for?: Henry. According to Geoff Lumb's authoritative 1999 history of the company (an Ian Allan publication), his father worked for the North Eastern Railway. Charles Henry became a draughtsman with the rolling stock (later bus and tram) builder Charles Roberts in Wakefield and went on to work for RET Construction, successor to the Rail-less Electric Traction trolleybus company. He then set up on his own in 1917, building bus and tram bodies and in 1921 moved this within Leeds from Hunslet to Crossgates, where the company remained to the end of its days.
All plain sailing?: Although it seems to have been successful in picking up orders for its innovative composite bodies right from the start, there were some financial problems along the way. In 1922, debts forced the original company into liquidation and a successor company, Charles H Roe (1923) Ltd took over the following year and was renamed without the date 11 years later. By then, the company was about to take some important steps forward.
In what way?: It had long enjoyed a close relationship with Leeds City Transport and in 1935 produced its first patented safety staircase for its principal client. The feature – first shown in a streamlined, fully-fronted AEC Regent – had two intermediate landings at right angles, and a long straight main section. Over 700 were supplied to various operators before the patents expired in 1950 and it remained a Roe feature after that.
What became of the company?: It was courted by potential buyers. In 1939, English Electric and Metro-Cammell Weymann both made approaches, but one world war and eight years elapsed before a

takeover was effected. There had also been talk of a merger with Mumford, the Gloucestershire bodybuilder, but it was Park Royal Vehicles that took over in July 1947. Less than two years later, in April 1949, Park Royal joined AEC, Crossley and Maudslay in the Associated Commercial Vehicles group. The founder stepped down as managing director in 1952 and finally retired as chairman in September 1962. By then, ACV had 'merged' ('been taken over by' was nearer the truth) with Leyland and more change was on its way.
What was that?: In 1965, Leyland bought a 25% stake in the state-owned Eastern Coach Works and Bristol businesses, while the Transport Holding Company took a 30% stake in Park Royal and Roe. In 1969, after THC's English and Welsh bus interests passed to the National Bus Company, these all became 50% Leyland/50% NBC companies and that remained the case until Leyland took 100% control in 1982.
How did these changes affect Roe?: Its older products remained largely unaffected. A composite Roe body retained its distinctive look right up to 1969, when the last rear entrance Daimler CVG6s went to Northampton. But Park Royal rapidly transferred production of metal-framed bodies into Leeds, with increasing elements of the parent company's designs becoming apparent. With the move to front entrance and/or rear-engined designs in the late-1950s, a standard Park Royal/Roe body appeared, although some of these still retained distinctive Roe features.
Why the and/or?: Because Roe bodied most of the few Guy Wulfrunians ever built. This front entrance/front-engined double-decker was designed for (and almost exclusively bought by) West Riding, hence the involvement of a local bodybuilder. There's an ironic ACV connection here as West Riding originally tried to have the chassis built by AEC, which perhaps wisely recognised that it might not work too well.
What happened after Leyland took control?: The 1970s saw the end of any meaningful difference between the products of Roe and Park Royal and some Yorkshire pride may have been massaged when Leyland's rationalisation saw it take its axe to Park Royal in 1980, while Roe kept going. In 1983, it was given the task of building the manufacturer's flagship Royal Tiger Doyen rear-engined coach, but it turned out to have swallowed the contents of a poisoned chalice.

Why was that?: It was unable to meet the quality and delivery standards expected by Leyland. In his book, 'Beyond Reality', Doug Jack explains that some of the drawings for the design were insufficiently accurate and Roe's skilled craftsmen were not permitted to make the necessary changes to the component parts. Production transferred to the bus assembly plant at Workington and, in a declining market for conventional buses, Roe was doomed to close. It shut in September 1984.
End of a glorious story?: Only the end of a glorious chapter. Miraculously, former plant director Russell Richardson bought the factory, relaunched it as a new company called Optare and the rest of that story is history.
Most notable Roe products?: Besides the Wulfrunians and the Leeds streamliner of 1935, there were 34 Mancunians for Selnec PTE in 1972 and, in 1952, Leeds ordered two Roe-bodied single-deck railcars for its yet-to-die tramway system.

Alan Millar

An impressive example of the coachbuilder's art, a 1934 Sunderland Corporation Daimler COG5 with centre entrance 46-seat body, no.27.

Gin a body meet a body

You too can have a body like mine, says MICHAEL DRYHURST – or a rebody. Or become the Governator of Califeernia . . .

In the post-WW2 period Beadle supplied many new bodies on refurbished postwar chassis to Southern/Western National, mainly on Bristol J, K and L types. What made these rebodyings interesting was the fact that their styling owed more to Eastern Coach Works design than to Beadle, as shown by Western National no.286, a 1939 K5G with postwar Beadle body. Although the cab is very Beadle, the rest is very ECW.

Photos: Michael Dryhurst

In the late 1940s Eastern Counties refurbished a number of elderly Leyland Titan TD2 – this included retro-fitting Gardner 5LW engines, Cov-Rad radiators and new Eastern Coach Works bodies to both highbridge and lowbridge layout. Highbridge no.AH11 is seen in Kings Lynn with its new all-metal ECW body.

IN EVERY WALK OF LIFE, WORLD WAR 2 brought with it many stresses and strains. For public road passenger services, WW2 brought in its wake previously unencountered and unimaginable problems, which were largely dealt with in the wartime make-do-and-mend spirit. In the aftermath of the war, there were possibly more problems to be addressed than during the conflict itself; the demand for, and pressures on, road passenger services reached new heights and while there had been a modicum of help in the form of the unfrozen and austerity buses allocated to companies during the war, there just weren't enough of these to cater for the tremendous immediate upsurge in postwar traffic.

There wasn't anything new in providing new bodies on older chassis – after all, doesn't the preserved Portsmouth Thornycroft J of 1919 carry a Dodson body of 1920, fitted in 1926? But if one reads all of those tomes dealing with the immediate postwar years, it would appear that new bodies were more readily available than new chassis. So why wait for a completely new bus if you had serviceable chassis whose original body was a little careworn but upon which could be built a new body? Many companies thought this way, and if the tolerant reader is expecting

a definitive history of which company rebodied what, then that would require to itself more space than is available here; hence this is in the nature of an overview, concerning itself more with the BET and Tilling/BET fleets of England and Wales rather than what was occurring north of the border. Why? Well, editor/guv advised steer clear unless you are 110% sure of your facts; facts stop somewhere around Alnwick . . . And the municipals.

It seems likely that the lengthening of a vehicle's life by providing it with a new body started during the dark days of WW2. Those AEC Regent I 662 and Leyland Titan TD1/2 of the early 1930s had sturdy chassis while the same cannot be said of the bodies supplied originally; given the increased traffic versus vehicle shortages caused by wartime circumstance, the perceived wisdom was to rebody those earlier stalwart chassis. While many saloons were so rebodied during WW2, double-deckers were to be rebodied by a number of companies, such as Alexander, Beadle, Brush, Croft, East Lancs, Eastern Coach Works, Northern Coachbuilders, Roe and Willowbrook, and even London Transport itself built bodies to austerity specification in both highbridge and lowbridge form, albeit to prewar styling; in fact, of the foregoing, while

Above: Beadle was one of a number of companies that supplied utility bodywork, although not to austerity look. Here on a 1931 AEC Regent I is a 1944-built Beadle body to the company's then-standard six-bay layout. It is no.6272 in the Brighton Hove & District fleet and is seen laying-over at Hove station in February 1953.

Left: The Red & White group long had Lydney Coachworks as its in-house bodybuilder. By the mid-1950s the bodywork on many of the company's early postwar buses was in a very poor state and a rebuild programme was decided on. This was to have been undertaken by Lydney but that company hit difficult times and the work was transferred to the bodybuilding shops of Bristol Tramways. Not unnaturally, the bodies had an ECW look. Red & White no.S1247, an Albion Valkyrie CX13 is seen at Chepstow bus station in August 1958.

Above: Although most postwar rebodying was on Leyland Titan chassis, an exception was this batch of Devon General AEC Regent I, originally built in 1934 with Short Bros bodies. In 1949 new bodies were built on the chassis by Brush, like DR212, seen in Paul Street bus station, Exeter, on Christmas Eve 1953. Note the rear wheeltrim, common on DG's AEC fleet. Many of these Brush rebodies were later converted to open-toppers, lasting as such until 1960/1.

Right: A number of Bristol G and K types received new postwar bodies by ECW, most of the highbridge examples going to Bristol Tramways. Seen in August 1958 is no.C3406, a K6A. The styling of the cab window is interesting; was this a new body fitted originally to a GO5G and subsequently fitted to this K6A?

the construction was of austerity specification the wartime styling of bodies by Beadle, East Lancs and ECW didn't have that utility look.

As mentioned earlier, the bulk of the post-WW2 rebodying programme was undertaken by constituent companies of the BET and BTC (formerly Tilling) groupings; of the latter, it was inevitable that the bulk would be on Bristol chassis, although there was a significant number on both AEC and Leyland as well, not surprising given the Tilling/BAT break-up in 1942. But of the BET constituent companies that embarked

In the postwar period Burlingham was involved in providing new bodywork on prewar chassis, most notably on the Leyland Tiger TS series, supplying both BET and BTC fleets. This was one of a number supplied to the Lincolnshire Road Car company and no.1439 is seen at Grantham bus station in October 1959.

Right: A highbridge version of the ECW body style fitted to rebodied Bristol Ks was supplied to Eastern Counties, mainly on what had been utility chassis. LKH36, a 1945 bus, by now with Gardner 5LW engine and 8ft-wide body, is seen in Peterborough in April 1958.

Below: For its York-West Yorkshire fleet, the West Yorkshire Road Car company drastically rebuilt some 1938/9 Bristol K5G, including fitting new ECW KS-style bodies. Such was the extent of the rebuilding that only by studying the wheel hubs/axles could it be determined that these were of prewar origin.

Southdown embarked on a rebodying programme in the 1946-50 period, involving 152 chassis of Leyland types TD3, TD4 and TD5 and employing five bodybuilding firms. Sixteen new bodies were supplied by Northern Counties, all to this distinctive and unmistakably NCME style. Built with a torque converter, and this originally a TD4c with Beadle body, no.148 is seen in its new guise in Old Steine, Brighton, in May 1958.

Left: South-east England was truly a BET stronghold with East Kent, Maidstone & District and Southdown (plus BTC's Brighton Hove & District and a trio of municipal operators). Like Southdown, East Kent embarked on a rebodying programme of its Leyland TD4 and TD5 buses, involving some 60 chassis. All received lowbridge bodies by ECW or Park Royal and one of the latter, JG 9521, is seen in the shadow of the White Cliffs of Dover.

Below: Yorkshire Traction was another BET affiliate which undertook a rebodying programme of prewar buses, again based on the sturdy Titan. This is a TD4, no.722L, with a postwar Roe lowbridge body. It is seen in Doncaster in August 1958, with Rossie Motors' Barnard-bodied Daimler CVD6 behind.

upon a large-scale rebodying programme in the postwar period, the vast majority of these were based on the Leyland Titan chassis, usually of the TD3/TD4/TD5 sub-types. Interesting . . .

South-east England was a hotbed of double-decker rebodying. While Maidstone & District set about a complete rebodying of its Bristol, Daimler and Guy utility buses, fellow BET constituents, East Kent and Southdown, had many of their postwar Leylands rebodied; with East Kent, TD4 chassis would receive new bodywork by either ECW or Park Royal. Southdown, however, embarked on a programme of rebodying over 150 TD3/TD4/TD5 chassis in the period 1946-50; five companies were involved in this massive operation, Beadle, East Lancs, Park Royal, Northern Counties and Saunders, and many of these rebodied buses survived in Southdown service until the early 1960s, a testament to the soundness of the rebodying programme and the robustness of the Leyland chassis. I can well remember many of these

Left: Maidstone & District received a large number of austerity and semi-austerity buses. While there were Daimler CW and Guy Arab chassis, the vast majority of these were based on the Bristol K6A. With the exception of one Saunders body to basic RT style, all of M&D's austerity fleet was rebodied by Weymann, including the only Orion style bodies to be built on Bristol chassis. This is DH23, a Guy Arab II supplied in 1943, with a 1952-built Weymann body, seen in Maidstone in 1961 alongside DL13, a 1949 Bristol K6A with lowbridge Weymann body – with a nearside wing from an earlier Bristol.

In 1938 the North Western Road Car company received some 65 Bristol K5G chassis, bodied mostly by ECW. In 1951/2 these chassis were refurbished extensively, then to be fitted with new Willowbrook lowbridge bodies, becoming a familiar sight in the north west. This is no.415, a 1938 K5G, at Piccadilly bus station, Manchester, one quiet Sunday in August 1958.

Although it was located close to the Weymann works at Addlestone, the preferred supplier of double-deck bodies to Aldershot & District was Blackburn-based East Lancs. Although A&D had some of its utility Guys rebodied by Weymann, perhaps the most interesting rebodies were those by East Lancs, which in 1954 built 8ft-wide lowbridge bodies on 1945 Guy Arab II chassis.

Southdown 'rebods' running alongside brand-new Titan PD3 Queen Marys, and in 1961 a quartet of these Southdown 'rebods' was sold to Brighton Corporation for further service.

I'm on dinner duty this evening. In return for the lady-wife re-seeding the lawn, washing the tractor and chasing away the deer, I'm charged with sautéing the fish and scallops, topping them with tomatoes and onions, and laying them in a bed of shrimp soup laced with garlic. Which tends to put on the back-burner – forgive the analogy – those Potteries TD4s that

received the magnificent new bodies by Northern Counties in 1951 that were in such a fine state that they were subsequently placed on to PD-series chassis.

And which bodybuilding companies were in the vanguard of that postwar programme? Brush did its bit, as did Strachans, but those that spring to mind most readily are ECW, and ECW … and, well, ECW. The formation of the British Transport Commission encompassed not only bus-operating companies but also the manufacturing entities of Bristol and ECW. Theoretically, the only recipients of ECW bodywork

During the war Alexander had built utility double-deck bodies on AEC Regal and Leyland Tiger saloons for SMT Group companies and after the war built bodies to Leyland's standard design on Titan PD1 chassis. Alexander also built new bodies for Ribble on refurbished Titan TD4 chassis, like no.2059, seen at Blackburn in August 1958. Note the similarity of the Alexander product to contemporary Leyland designs.

were those companies within the BTC fold, but beyond the 1948 cut-off date ECW had unfulfilled orders that were placed well before then, and delivered well after, such as the Maidstone & District Bristol L6A/ECWs, most of which did not arrive at Knightrider Street until well into 1950. So how many BET affiliates specified bodies by BTC-associated ECW on their refurbished chassis? Off the top of me 'ead (never to be trusted) East Kent, East Yorkshire (highbridge to Beverley Bar style), Northern General, Ribble and NGT-associate Tynemouth all took ECW bodies on refurbished chassis. Cumberland had rebodied TD4 chassis by Burlingham and ECW, both to lowbridge layout. In addition to the ECW rebodies, Ribble took new bodies on existing double-deck chassis by Alexander and Burlingham. Also there was considerable rebodying of prewar Leyland Tiger chassis, with new coach bodies by Duple and Windover, while Burlingham and Roe, among others, delivered bus bodywork.

The North Western Road Car company postwar rebodying programme can probably justify a complete article – but, sorry, I think I've got to go and check the oven. Hopefully the pictures can speak for themselves . . . **CB**

A shot in the dark

JOHN ROBINSON reveals some of the secrets of successful night photography

I WAS SOME FIVE YEARS INTO MY INTEREST in bus photography before I photographed a bus at night. I had always admired the after-dark masterpieces of photographers such as Geoff Atkins and Tom Moore that had graced the pages of books and magazines but had never bothered trying it for myself.

Killing time in a rainy Cardiff waiting for a day excursion train back to Birmingham one Sunday in November 1977 it suddenly struck me that I was standing in a busy bus station and I had all the equipment I needed to take some night photographs, having brought a tripod with me for some depot shots earlier in the day.

I instinctively sped into action and began to photograph the various occupants of Cardiff's Central

In 1979 Lancashire United received 23 Leyland Nationals. Although it was still operating separately from the parent Greater Manchester fleet, following LUT's takeover in 1976, these buses were among the first to be delivered in a modified version of GMT's standard orange/white livery with Lancashire United Transport fleetnames. No.546 stands at Bewsey Street terminus, Wigan, in December 1980; on 31 March the following year LUT was fully absorbed into GMT and its identity gradually disappeared.

Photos: John Robinson

Bus Station. Droplets of water on the lens caused by the persistent rain meant that most of the pictures were rejects as light was reflected in these droplets resulting in strange circular patterns being exposed on to the film. Lesson one was learnt – keep the lens dry and clean! While this should always be the case anyway, in daylight you might just get away with not doing it but at night it is a different matter as any foreign bodies on the lens such as water or dirt create these strange effects as light is hitting the lens from a number of sources and directions.

However, I was fortunate that a couple of the photographs were okay and thus my expedition into the world of night photography began.

At this time the shutter speed settings on cameras I was using only went down to 1 second, with any longer exposures being made using the bulb (B) setting. This caused problems in obtaining a meter reading as the camera's meter, and my hand-held meter, were unable to give any sort of reading in the very low light associated with night photography. This meant that an educated guess was usually required, although sometimes it was possible to alter the film speed setting on the camera to its maximum value to fool the light meter into giving a reading, and then calculate the exposure back to the lower film speed in use. Usually, though, it was quicker to guess than carry out

Right: Among the first night photographs John took of buses on that day trip to Cardiff in November 1977 was Tyne & Wear PTE no.119, a 1963 Weymann-bodied Leyland Atlantean, one of a number of buses on hire to City of Cardiff Transport at the time.

Below: After specifying Alexander Y type bodywork for several batches of AEC Reliances between 1964 and 1975, Premier Travel, Cambridge, turned to Plaxton to body four Reliances in 1975. The lighting of Digbeth Coach Station, Birmingham, highlights a dramatic pattern of tyre tracks on the oily floor in this February 1979 view of no.254.

Seen in Pool Meadow, Coventry, after arrival from Nuneaton is Midland Red no.5905, a BMMO S22; it was one of 37 similar buses new in 1968 with BMMO 45-seat bodywork. Originally dual-purpose vehicles, they had been downgraded to bus status by February 1979, when this photo was taken.

mental arithmetic on the spot as by the time the calculation was completed the bus may well have moved off!

With guesswork the vast majority of my photographs were satisfactorily exposed, using an exposure based on approximately 5 seconds at f5.6 on 125ASA film for typical town centre lighting. I never bracketed (that is, took a number of identical shots at different exposures to increase the chance of one being correct) as in those days I was not aware of this technique; even if I had been, I could not have afforded to burn up film in this way on a student grant!

In later years I used cameras with shutter speeds going down to 30 seconds, which meant that the camera's light meter was always able to give me an accurate reading at night, thus speeding up the picture-taking process. The only downside of this was that while it was possible to shield the lens during a bulb exposure if anything unwanted, such as a car or pedestrian, crossed the field of view, this was not possible with a fixed exposure time, so if anything went wrong the picture had to be re-taken.

Light readings have to be taken from the bus itself to avoid being influenced by bright light sources such as streetlights, headlights and illuminated buildings, otherwise the subject matter would be underexposed and the picture unsatisfactory.

It is obviously important to select locations where buses will be stopped for long enough to set up and take the picture, which invariably means bus stations and street loading points or, if you work quickly, at traffic lights. Depots, of course, are another suitable place.

A sturdy tripod is absolutely necessary for night photography to ensure the camera is solidly supported and a cable release enables the shutter to be released smoothly without vibrating the camera – and thus ruining the picture.

Around 1983 I changed from Ilford FP4 125ASA film to the same manufacturer's XP2 400ASA stock which I found to give particularly good results at night. Being a faster film (that is, with greater sensitivity to light) the exposures were shorter – especially useful for pictures at traffic lights – and also this particular film had a lot more latitude. I already had the record shot 'in the bag' – taken in daylight – so I could be more adventurous when taking pictures at night.

I have always felt that the best night shots are those which have an air of 'mystery' rather than simply showing all the detail which would appear in a similar photograph taken in daylight. I have therefore tended to strive for atmospheric pictures where shadows and reflections off wet roads and pavements and illuminated buildings, were integral aspects of the composition. Steamed-up bus windows with figures visible behind them were a bonus whenever they could be obtained.

Unique to Warrington were its 12 7ft 6in-wide Leyland Titan PD2/40 Specials with East Lancs forward entrance bodies, new in 1965. No.49 stands at the crew changeover point in Winwick Street in January 1981 on route 79, Warrington's last crew-operated route. Its conversion to driver-only operation two months later led to the demise of the Titans.

In the earlier years I would often ask drivers to turn off their headlights – just leaving their sidelights on – as this avoided glare from the headlights burning out the surrounding area on the photograph. Later, when I invested in a powerful hammerhead flashgun I found that photographing buses with their headlights on, but firing the flashgun directly at them on maximum power during the exposure, produced better results as the burning-out effect was considerably reduced.

This was done, of course, only on buses which were stationary long enough for me to advise the driver of my intention and with their approval. 'Open flash' as this technique is known, is also useful for illuminating parts of the bus which are in shadow, normally the front end, and also makes the drivers more visible, assuming they stay motionless for the duration of the exposure, as requested!

I only took black-and-white night photographs for the first three years, and when I tried my hand at using colour transparency film for night photographs I was very pleased with the results, the night effect in colour being very dramatic in a lot of cases.

The air suspension and, often, kneeling capabilities of modern buses, has made today's night photography more difficult as the bodywork of the ostensibly stationary bus is prone to move during the exposure, causing the subject to be rendered unsharp. There also tends to be much more traffic and many more people – some not too desirable in this day and age – in towns at night than there used to be as town centre facilities stay open later, adding to the difficulties of photography.

Ironically, I have found that generally the best time to take night shots now is actually in the early morning in the winter months as there tends to be less traffic, and certainly fewer people, allowing pictures to be taken unhindered. **CB**

Left: **Blackpool's subterranean Talbot Road bus station is the setting for this October 1983 view of Blackpool no.503, one of a batch of 25 Metro-Cammell-bodied Leyland Titan PD3A/1s placed in service in 1967.**

Below: **Caught in stationary traffic taking a party through the Blackpool Illuminations in October 1983 is Fylde Borough no.95, a Northern Counties-bodied Leyland Atlantean, dating from 1979.**

Above: Standing outside Manchester Piccadilly station operating the Centreline service in March 1984 is Greater Manchester no.1724, one of the Seddon Pennine IV:236 Midis with Pennine coachwork. These buses were associated with this service for many years until replaced in the mid-1980s by Dennis Dominos.

Below: Nottingham was known for the individualistic design of the bodywork it specified on rear-engined chassis. A trio of Nottingham standard bodies are seen in this January 1985 view in Angel Row in the city centre: nearest the camera is Daimler Fleetline no.200 with Leyland Atlantean no.637 behind and Fleetline no.215 bringing up the rear. The Fleetlines carry Northern Counties bodies and the Atlantean almost identical bodywork by East Lancs.

Above: Yorkshire Traction no.251, a Duple Dominant-bodied Leyland Leopard in National Express white coach livery awaits departure for Doncaster from Chorlton Street coach station, Manchester, in February 1985.

Below: Selnec PTE, and its successor Greater Manchester Transport, standardised on Leyland Atlanteans and Daimler Fleetlines with Northern Counties or Park Royal bodywork for the majority of its double-deck requirements from 1972 to 1984. Waiting at traffic lights in Manchester's London Road in February 1985 is Atlantean no.8627, showing the final, light alloy, version of the PTE's standard Northern Counties bodywork.

Standing in the melting snow at Hanley bus station in January 1986 is PMT Leyland National no.284, one of a batch new in 1975.

For decades until the run-up to deregulation, Mayne had been the only independent stage carriage operator based in Manchester, a situation that dramatically changed as the city became overrun with new operators. Loading in Piccadilly in March 1987 is LRJ 212P, one of five Roe-bodied Daimler Fleetlines bought new in 1976. Behind is Carlyle-bodied Sherpa D186 NON of United Transport's Bee Line Buzz Company, which had launched an intensive network of minibus services in Stockport and South Manchester with a fleet of 225 vehicles two months before this photo was taken.

No.4:
The Midland Red break-up

When: 6 September 1981

What happened?: The Midland Red Omnibus Company – Birmingham & Midland Motor Omnibus Company until 1974 – was broken up into five separate companies, Midland Red (North), Midland Red (South), Midland Red (East), Midland Red (West) and Midland Red (Express), while the Carlyle Works in Edgbaston became a free-standing unit.

Why?: Because this once profitable bus company – a jewel in the crown of the BET group – had become one of the financial black holes within the National Bus Company.

What caused that to happen?: It lost its best markets. Until 3 December 1973, it ran an intensive network of services in Birmingham, Coventry and the Black Country in addition to a mix of urban, interurban and rural routes across Staffordshire, Worcestershire, Herefordshire, Shropshire, Warwickshire and Leicestershire. Its combined fleet totalled around 1,900 and the intensive urban routes cross-subsidised the rural routes. That fateful day in 1973 saw NBC sell 413 buses, six garages and the Birmingham, Coventry and Black Country routes to the West Midlands PTE.

Why did it do that?: The PTEs had been set up four years earlier with a remit to provide what the legislation described as a properly efficient, integrated public passenger transport service. One of their models was London Transport, which had bought up – compulsorily – every bus operator in its area in 1933. Selnec PTE had already bought the best bits of North Western Road Car to reduce the overlap with its own former municipal buses and West Midlands persuaded NBC to do the same with Midland Red. There was a tiny *quid pro quo* as a few PTE routes beyond the West Midlands County boundary (such as former Wolverhampton Corporation services into rural Staffordshire) went to Midland Red in exchange.

And the end result of this was?: That Midland Red's sums didn't add up. It lost the best means of cross-subsidising its marginal or loss-making routes and the smaller company still had a head office

and central works in Birmingham. The other end result was that NBC never sold another PTE-area bus company. It bent over backwards to work in partnership with the other PTEs, but selling good businesses was off its agenda.

Did it do anything else?: It tried to plug the black hole at Midland Red by acquiring other urban operators. In Staffordshire, it bought Harper Brothers of Heath Hayes (which ran pale green double-deckers into Birmingham) and Green Bus of Rugeley, while it set out to buy up the clutch of independents serving Telford new town. They may have helped stem the losses, but this was far from enough to compensate for what had gone. It also had to go cap in hand to the local authorities to seek support for its loss-making routes.

And it began a quest for viability?: Certainly did. What turned out to be two of the most significant moves were the appointment of one of John Hargreaves as general manager and Brian Barratt as assistant traffic manager (planning), both in 1974. John Hargreaves moved on to become a highly influential regional director in 1977 (of which more later) while Brian Barratt developed the Viable Network Project.

Which was?: A system that harnessed computer power to analyse the costs of different routes and establish how much revenue each one generated. This may sound basic stuff, but it was a new concept for the bus industry. And while you may never have heard about VNP, you're more likely to know the name by which it soon became known across NBC.

And that was?: MAP. Market Analysis Project. It was with MAP that NBC was able to match its services more closely to perceived demand and provide the information that the county councils expected if they were to cough up the readies to keep the likes of Midland Red afloat. At Midland Red, it also led to the start of local branding, with names like Reddibus, Tellus and Hotspur adopted for revamped networks.

So where does John Hargreaves come back into the story?: The fleet had shrunk to 860 as individual buses were worked much harder, but what was known a little euphemistically as a 'revenue shortfall' ('loss' to you and me) had quadrupled in two years to 1980, was projected to top £5 million in 1981/82 and the best the company could expect in revenue support was about £2.3 million. The Hargreaves solution was to separate the company from the high overheads of its head office and central works, divide the remaining buses between the five new operating companies closer to the markets they served and provide admin support from neighbouring companies Potteries, Trent, United Counties and Bristol Omnibus.

What happened next?: It was deemed so successful that John Hargreaves applied the same formula across most of the other companies in his southern region of NBC. Midland Red (East) later renamed itself Midland Fox and the Express company was integrated into Midland Red (West). The four companies went separate ways on privatisation and only First still has a company (the former West business) with Midland Red in its official title. Not that it's allowed to project it to the outside world, as FirstSpeak deems this to be First in Wyvern. Wherever that is.

Greatest myth?: That the split-up was a preparation for privatisation. It was undertaken long before that was a serious item on the Thatcher government's agenda and longer still before it was decreed that NBC would be broken up for sale.

Alan Millar

Following the split-up of Midland Red, the new Midland Red North company applied local identities to its fleet using coloured bands on the standard NBC red – Mercian was green, Hotspur was blue and, as here, Chaserider was maroon. Seen at Cannock garage in September 1982 is no.6158, a 1969 Daimler Fleetline with Alexander body.
Gavin Booth

Weymann – th

ALAN TOWNSIN delves into the history and products of one of Britain's best-loved coachbuilders

Contrasting examples of Weymann bodies on AEC chassis, both in the fleet of J Bullock & Sons, of Featherstone, trading as B&S, are seen here in Leeds in late 1935. The lowbridge 8.8-litre Regent, no.149 dating from April 1933, had 52-seat composite body no.C526 conforming to the standard Weymann double-deck style of the period. Behind it, Q-type single-decker no.161 had 'flexible' 39-seat body W994, one of a pair new in June 1934. The latter was built to one of AEC's registered styles for this side-engined model. B&S was taken over by West Riding in 1950 but both vehicles had been withdrawn by then.

Photos: Alan Townsin collection, except as stated.

JOHN SENIOR'S TEXT IN THE BOOK 'THE Weymann Story, Part One – 1923-1945', published in 2002 by Venture Publications, concentrates on the firm's business history. He suggests that the ownership of Weymann's between 1925 and 1937 by a South African gold mining concern 'must, surely, arouse the curiosity of even the most diehard nuts-and-bolts bus enthusiast', I suspect with me most in mind.

Accepting that description with a degree of pride – it is now 50 years since I wrote an article about Weymann in *Buses Illustrated* – and leavened by a mainly engineering-based career spent in and around the industry, I do feel there is much to be said on the 'nuts and bolts' side of any manufacturer's story. The design features, the reasons and people behind them had immense influence on that of Weymann, as I seek

to outline here. I have also not forgotten that it was John Senior, still himself surely a bus enthusiast at heart, who made history by first seeing the possibilities for well-illustrated large-page books on the subject –

nuts and b⬡lts

indeed I have enjoyed filling quite a few of them, very largely from that angle.

In my view it was the quality of Weymann's products, especially from 1933 and coupled with very effective sales policy, that allowed it to climb from a weak position to a much stronger one, with an enviable list of regular customers. The firm became saleable and when circumstances not related to its activities led to it being sold in 1937 to Prudential Assurance, this approach, as well as the success, continued largely undisturbed.

To me, possibly the most intriguing aspect of the Weymann story is the way in which the pursuit of flexibility on which Charles Terres Weymann based his original design for car bodies soon gave way to an almost completely opposite approach in the MCW metal-framed bus body, as built either by Metro-Cammell or Weymann, among the most rigid of bus body designs.

Aviator

Weymann was an aviator, joining the French Air Force in World War 1, and hence familiar with the wood-and-canvas structure of early aircraft, lightly constructed yet flexible enough to avoid catastrophic breakage when subjected to sudden air gusts. He saw that the wood-framed car body of that era was also subjected to distortion; the stiff road springs caused the chassis to twist and the body was incapable of resisting. Weymann's patented flexible body used light metal brackets to connect the wooden frame parts while keeping them apart, thus eliminating squeaks and rattles – leathercloth covering helped to allow the desired flexibility.

Weymann's factories in Paris and London then merely supplied the brackets to bodybuilders building the bodies under licence. By 1928 it was claimed that there were some 50,000 car bodies of Weymann's patent design in use in the two countries, the top end

It was Metro-Cammell that had brought its very successful form of metal-framed construction to the joint MCW set-up. It had evolved this standard style of double-decker, supplied to several municipal fleets with very little change from 1934, remaining in production until 1940 and again from 1946 to 1951. This example was one of 24 on Leyland Titan TD4c chassis for Wallasey Corporation dating from early 1937.

of the range on Bentley or equivalent marques, bodied by firms such as Vanden Plas. Weymann opened bodybuilding works of its own in 1925, the British one initially at Putney but in 1928 it moved to larger premises in Addlestone, near Weybridge, Surrey (where it was to remain until closure in 1966). Ironically, the fabric-covered car body was slipping out of favour, lacking the appeal of high-gloss paintwork and, despite the compromise use of metal panelling below the waist, demand began to drop.

By early 1929 the Weymann patented design was being applied to a few coaches and buses. For them, the side framing used metal strips secured by five small bolts at every junction between horizontal rails and pillars. Such a 'flexible' body was virtually as rigid as one with conventional joints, especially if metal-panelled except for the roof, as was soon usual.

The body numbers quoted in PSV Circle body number lists imply that the 15 bus and coach bodies built in 1929 formed only about 6% of the total output that year. The first order from a major operator came from the Scottish Motor Traction Co Ltd, for two 32-seat bus bodies on Maudslay ML3 chassis, delivered in October. The number built crept up to 20 in 1930, mostly for independent operators, and building under

Weymann's interpretation of what was broadly a similar outline, using the same type of metal framing, was different in proportions and numerous detail features – it too was adopted as a standard, being supplied to many of the firm's customers in the 1934-7 period and continuing in a few cases, most notably Liverpool, until some of the last shells of this outline (for which the ordered AEC chassis were not built) were used up on wartime Guy Arab chassis. The example shown, Bradford Corporation no.425 on AEC Regent 7.7-litre chassis with body M819, dated from September 1936. The more rounded rear-end is perhaps the most obvious difference from the Met-Camm version but Weymann favoured shallower windows with deeper ceiling cove panels within and the roof construction was quite different, with the framing exposed. Other Weymann 'trademarks' included the more rounded form of the projecting cab front, the style of ventilator in the front dome panel and the well-radiused top corners of both the lower deck rear window and the emergency window upstairs. The shape of the louvres over the side windows was a Bradford feature, intended to draw rain drips well clear.

licence from Weymann's also spread to this field in a few cases but, with the car side in sharp decline, prospects must have looked bleak.

A breakthrough to a more secure future came with the securing of an order for 25 coach bodies on AEC Regal chassis from Green Line Coaches Ltd, then part

The trend to a curved frontal profile was at first met very simply by applying this feature to the upperworks of an otherwise unchanged body, adopted for some customers from 1937 although the effect with the prominent projecting cab front was only mildly different. This example with body M952 is one of the 62 AEC Regents purchased for the replacement of trams in Swansea and originally owned by the Swansea Tramways & Improvements Co, although it was taken into the main South Wales Transport Co Ltd fleet when seen in 1952 – several of the batch completed 20 years in service.
Roy Marshall

of the Underground group to which the London General Omnibus Co Ltd also belonged, the latter designing the bodies, of conventional composite construction. It was then the biggest bus or coach order Weymann had built, quite apart from the prestige of gaining such a customer, and may well have ensured Weymann's survival. Prompt delivery in early 1931 was essential and the ability to achieve it was probably due to W R Black (later Sir William and then Lord Black, of the ACV and Leyland empires), who had joined Weymann's as general manager in 1928, already experienced in quantity production from his earlier career with Vickers Ltd, the engineering group, whose bodybuilding department at Crayford he had managed – it was closed in 1929.

Bodies of coachbuilt (composite) construction, immediately more strongly in demand, were given a separate numbering series beginning at C1. The hitherto plain numbering series for bodies to Weymann's patent design later received a W prefix. Weymann built 88 bus and coach bodies in 1931, largely coachbuilt, including the first few Weymann double-deckers. It was agreed in January 1932 to cease car body output and at that point C T Weymann resigned.

An upsurge of orders in 1931/2 reflected the arrival of B Homfray Davies (not a hyphenated name, incidentally) as sales director, playing a major role in the immense expansion that followed. Weymann's total output in 1932 of 206 bus bodies, mostly composite,

was more than double that for 1931, at a time when the depression was making such progress rare. Another key figure, joining the firm's design team in 1931, was Harold Cook, later appointed chief draughtsman and, by early wartime, chief engineer – soon styles identifiable on sight as Weymann products began to appear.

The setting-up of MCW

The key turning point came in July 1932 with an agreement between the Metropolitan-Cammell Carriage Wagon and Finance Co Ltd and Weymann's Motor Bodies (1925) Ltd, jointly setting up Metropolitan-Cammell-Weymann Motor Bodies Ltd, better-known as MCW, to handle sales and share technical expertise. Metropolitan-Cammell (often called Metro-Cammell, Met-Camm or MCCW – the 'Finance' part of the title was dropped in 1934) had

extensive works in Birmingham – it was itself the result of a merger in January 1929 of several railway rolling-stock builders hitherto owned either by Vickers or the Cammell Laird engineering group. Among its best customers was the Underground group in London.

Metro-Cammell decided to apply its expertise in metal-framed railway carriages to bus work; development began in 1929, with Colin Bailey and Freddy Rayer as leading lights, the latter as designer. In 1930 two prototype double-deck bodies were built, for Birmingham Corporation and the LGOC; MCCW output of 59 bus bodies in 1931 was largely for these organisations.

The share capital of MCW was split 60:40 between Metro-Cammell and Weymann. All orders henceforth went via MCW, which had offices in the Vickers group's London headquarters, with Homfray Davies in charge of sales. In his text, John Senior puts emphasis on an agreement between Metro-Cammell and Weymann requiring output also to be split 60:40. Achieving this precisely would have been very difficult and later evidence implies some flexibility.

In several respects, the two bodybuilding concerns retained far more independence than was implied by the public 'face' of MCW, which controlled advertising and publicity, effective **sales** force though it certainly

was. Significantly, until wartime, the maker's nameplates gave the full names of the respective bodybuilders, neither version quoting the MCW name. Metro-Cammell used a bronze casting with the lettering having a simulated woven background, usually attached to the staircase side, whereas Weymann's used a simpler style of brass plate.

Interestingly, after the MCW sales office was moved out of central London to Addlestone in wartime, the concern's utility double-deckers, all built by Weymann's, carried a new and rather ambiguous plate, very like the prewar MCCW version in appearance, but reading 'Bodywork incorporating Metro-Cammell-Weymann patented composite construction'. This continued on Weymann's postwar bodies, with reference to either metal or composite, although Metro-Cammell continued to use its prewar type of plate with its own full name. Another reflection of their separate status was that Metro-Cammell and Weymann each continued to have their own stands at shows right through to 1964, though they were adjacent and laid out to be used as one.

Evolution of the Weymann look

Both concerns retained their own design departments and, except where working to customers' specifications

The major styling breakthrough came in 1938 with the adoption of the smooth gently-curving profile, with distinctive treatment of the upper deck corner pillars. Among the first large-scale applications was the completely new Brighton Corporation fleet of Weymann-bodied vehicles with which that undertaking replaced its trams in spring 1939. This scene at the Old Steine dated from early May, no.3 being one of the 44 AEC 661T trolleybuses with metal-framed bodies, this one being M1919. Alongside is no.71, one of 11 of the 21 AEC Regent 8.8-litre buses that had composite bodies, in this case C5389. The general manager at Brighton had specified that the glazing on these and the ten generally similar buses with metal-framed bodies (one of which is the famous FUF 63, happily still in good order) was to be interchangeable and thus their appearance was almost identical, very rarely so between Weymann bodies of the two forms of construction. The new services were jointly operated with the Brighton Hove & District company which received some almost identical trolleybuses, one of the very few cases of Weymann supplying a Tilling company. They were delivered later in the year but the war delayed their use until 1945/6.

specifying otherwise, their products usually remained instantly identifiable, very possibly reflecting the judgement of Freddy Rayer at MCCW and Harold Cook at Weymann.

Weymann metal-framed bodies began to be built early in 1933 – a new numbering series for them began at M1. Although the structural design, standardised pillar section and hot-riveted construction were all as used by Metro-Cammell, the overall body designs were handled in the Addlestone drawing office. Weymann established its own standard metal-framed body outlines from the outset, tending to adopt more flowing curves than favoured by Metro-Cammell, notably around the rear dome and the style of protruding cab front panel then usual. There were some similarities to the firm's composite styles but the metal version tended to have bolder lines, double-deckers having five bays between bulkheads instead of the more usual six on the composite.

Management changes, with some influence on such matters as well as wider issues, began with the departure of Bill Black from Weymann in the summer of 1933, at first going to the smaller firm, J C Beadle, at Dartford (making one wonder why he left Weymann) before going to Park Royal Coachworks in 1934. This was the year of what effectively was almost an exchange

of top people between Park Royal and Weymann for, after what amounted to a stop-gap appointment, Arthur Froggatt, who had been works manager at Park Royal, became general manager at Weymann's. Both men took various key people with them, and it was hardly coincidental that some of the two firms' products of the mid-1930s looked quite similar.

For me, the crowning glory of Weymann's artistic achievement was the double-deck style with unbroken curved profile as first built for some customers in 1938 and standardised for postwar production until the early 1950s. There had been earlier bodies of similar outline, notably from LPTB and Leyland, but Weymann combined this with its distinctive flowing treatment at the upper-deck front pillars. It was widely imitated and, for me, is what springs to mind at the mention of the Weymann name – sadly, today's double-deck body designers seem to have completely lost touch with the subtleties of that classic era. But does anyone know if it was Harold Cook or one of his staff who had the inspiration?

The process of quoting for an order required much work at whichever of the two works was chosen to build the bodies, if indeed the quotation was successful – the tendering process at municipalities made this by no means a forgone conclusion. Some operators'

A similarly sleek but rare design was produced for single-deckers, this example with metal-framed body M2108 being one of four AEC Regals supplied to Mansfield District Traction Co in 1940. This was one of the Balfour Beatty companies which were almost exclusively Weymann users. Unfortunately, at least in the writer's view, the postwar Weymann single-deck standard single-decker, of composite construction, adopted a rather strange design reverting to the idea of the canopy projecting beyond the windscreen, generally regarded as obsolete since about 1935, which appears to have been based on the preference of the East Midland company but was adopted for general home market use.

requirements were very detailed, often requiring additional work even if an existing basic design was acceptable. Hence, where a repeat order was involved, it was logical to put it to the same works.

There were further practical constraints, notably that any order for timber-framed bodies, whether or not of the Weymann flexible type, had to be built at Addlestone. By its nature more obviously an engineering works, Metro-Cammell was better equipped to deal with larger orders, making greater use of jigs than applied at Weymann's. Some customers expressed their own preferences and support for local industry was often an important factor in municipal choice. A useful lever to gaining orders in several such cases was willingness to supply body shells for completion locally, say in Liverpool's own workshops or by Mumford for Plymouth. The series of orders for the Cape Town Tramways company were all supplied by Weymann, as was to be expected in view of the financial links, but municipalities in South Africa were important Metro-Cammell customers.

'Met-Camm towns' and 'Weymann towns'

In practice, a distinct pattern emerged by the mid-1930s and, among municipal users, some towns and cities became Metro-Cammell strongholds and others Weymann, as conveyed by the list herewith relating to the 1932-9 period, when cross-overs from one to the other were very rare.

It was even more uncommon for both factories to supply one operator simultaneously, the main exception being Edinburgh, where in the 1935-9 period the double-deck orders went to Metro-Cammell while

the single-deckers were built by Weymann, in both cases metal-framed and on Daimler chassis. Prototypes and specialised types, such as the side-engined AEC Q, created their own rules, while Weymann handled all orders for small buses, such as Leyland Cubs.

The LGOC and then London Transport did not then adopt metal framing for its main bus fleet, mostly bodied at its Chiswick works, but did for the big trolleybus fleet built up from 1935, most of the big MCW contribution coming from Metro-Cammell, with smaller batches from Weymann. Several orders for bodywork for the 'green' country bus and related fleets were placed with Weymann, however, and following experience from 1933 with body M2, which was a replacement body for a Green Line AEC Regal, this was adopted for later prewar orders.

Weymann also dealt with most of the orders from company fleets, particularly so after 1934. A prominent exception was Midland Red – as well as being based in Birmingham, its size may have prompted the choice of

Metro-Cammell. However, in the 1930s the bodies supplied were mainly confined to double-deckers on that operator's own chassis in the 1932-36 period, a spin-off being a batch for Trent, which was a customer for Weymann composite bodies in 1937-40.

Most of the company orders came from parts of the British Electric Traction group. A sub-group were those companies that had come into that empire as offshoots of the National Electric Construction Co Ltd and Weymann regularly supplied all its bus-operating subsidiaries – Devon General; the City of Oxford company; Rhondda, and Western Welsh. Other concerns in the BET camp which were frequent customers in the 1930s included South Wales, Northern General, Maidstone & District and Potteries Motor Traction. BET Federation-design bodies were supplied to Western Welsh, Caledonian and Lincolnshire, the latter two under BET management at the time. A rather smaller group which gave almost all its bodywork contracts to Weymann was that of Balfour Beatty, then having several bus or trolleybus subsidiaries, mainly in the east midlands.

Orders for MCW from companies controlled or managed by Thomas Tilling Ltd were almost non-existent, such work normally going to Eastern Coach Works from within its own empire. Although MCW supplied all the Scottish municipal fleets of that era, quite an achievement in those days of local loyalties, company orders from north of the border were few. Metro-Cammell supplied batches to Central SMT and SMT itself in 1932/3, but here too the in-house Alexander bodybuilding department remained the usual first choice for the SMT group.

Proof of the pudding

The Weymann flexible bus body had continued in small-scale production, at an average rate of well under one per week, until the final five were built for Oxford in 1940 – it seems remarkable that output at so low a rate continued so long. The last traces of real flexibility were abandoned when the whole vehicle became metal-panelled, the concept effectively reducing to an alternative form of joint for the timber framing. However, a small loyal following remained, notably among the Oxford, PMT and Rhondda fleets, some examples retained until the mid-1950s, usually much rebuilt, though this was so of most composite bodies surviving as long. Weymann's conventional composite bodies mostly seemed about average in terms of durability, though Hull transferred a number of double-deckers to later chassis, implying that they perhaps used teak or similar framing.

Metal-framed bodywork was seen as an unknown quantity when MCW was formed in 1932. There had been earlier ventures, most notably that of Short Bros, mainly using light alloy, in the later 1920s but it had been only moderately successful; Birmingham Corporation, the largest user, reverted to composite for its 1931 batch of bodies from that firm. By contrast,

the Metro-Cammell and hence Weymann metal body seems to have been remarkably trouble-free from the start, but it took time to build up confidence. No one then had any idea that MCW metal bodies could give 20 years and more of service without major structural repair – it is noteworthy that rust in largely steel structures seems rarely to have been a problem.

In a curious inversion of the original Weymann principle, almost the only area of difficulty arose from flexing of the chassis, 'fighting' against the rigid body; body mountings allowing some relative movement eventually overcame this. A more radical approach led to MCW's pioneering applications of integral construction on trolleybuses for London Transport in 1938-40.

Few production figures are given in the Weymann book, and a diagram contradicts some of them, so I decided to make my own calculations of annual totals of the Weymann W, C and M series bodies and also those of Metro-Cammell (all metal-framed), from the beginning of production up to 1941. I worked from the PSV Circle body lists, themselves based on official records, and it has proved most enlightening. I have done my best to check the arithmetic carefully, but the yearly totals given in this way can be affected slightly by whether some individual dates given relate to delivery or first registration. Even so, the trends show up clearly.

In the early MCW period, there was rapid growth of output of metal-framed bodies at Weymann, from the modest start in 1933, with figures for 1934 and 1935 of 130 and 330 respectively, much as achieved slightly earlier at Metro-Cammell; total Weymann output was briefly slightly ahead in 1935. Then there was a spell of large-scale bus production at both factories in 1936-8, Weymann's total annual output running at over 500, save for 1937 when it dipped slightly below that figure, but reaching a peak in 1939 which I reckon to be 572. The metal-bodied share was dominant from 1934, running at over 400 per year, except again for a dip in 1937, although high composite body output that year partly compensated.

At Metro-Cammell, output reached 650 in 1936, also dipping slightly in 1937 but reaching 704 in 1938. The 1939 figure of 542 was down, dropping slightly below Weymann's, possibly due to that firm's involvement in tank production even before the outbreak of war. Weymann's figure for 1940 worked out at 289, compared to Met-Camm's 276. Both firms' bus output remained quite large until that autumn, when the war situation led to an almost complete national shut-down. The total bus body output of the two factories from the beginning up to that point was over 7,000. Of these, 6,000 were metal-framed, virtually all of which were then still in use, their trouble-free survival despite wartime neglect making an important contribution to the nation's transport system. Many were still in service into the 1950s and some even into the 1960s.

MCW as a joint operation had grown very rapidly

from its modest beginnings in 1932, when the combined annual output of the two firms was about 250 bodies, climbing to almost 1,200 in 1936 and above it in 1938. Weymann and Metro-Cammell had each reached the top league of British bus bodybuilders from 1935/6 onwards – together, they had become the strongest such organisation in Britain, the output figures underlining an achievement which I contend to have been based far more on design skill and craftsmanship than share deals, however exotic. **CB**

Major municipal MCW customers 1932-39
Those with fleets of over 100 MCW bodies in capitals

Metro-Cammell users	Weymann users	Weymann and Metro-Cammell user
BIRMINGHAM	LIVERPOOL	EDINBURGH
MANCHESTER	PLYMOUTH	
NOTTINGHAM	GLASGOW	Of the above, the only instances of
NEWCASTLE	Sheffield	Weymann bodies in the Metro-Cammell
SALFORD	Bradford	users' fleets were three Leyland Cubs at
Chesterfield	Hull	Chesterfield and an ex-demonstrator with
West Bromwich	Brighton	West Bromwich. The only Metro-Cammell body in the Weymann users'
Leicester	South Shields	fleets was an AEC Q at Bradford.
Coventry	Newport	

Annual Production figures for Weymann and Metro-Cammell, 1929-41
Bus, coach and trolleybus bodies (or shells for completion elsewhere)
Derived from PSV Circle body number lists (B1100, BB101-3, BB251 & BB252)

Year	Weymann flexible (W)	Weymann composite (C)	Weymann metal-framed (M)	Weymann total	Metro-Cammell metal-framed	MCW total
1929	15	-	-	15	-	-
1930	20	-	-	20	2	-
1931	26	62	-	88	59	-
1932	49	157	-	206	56	?
1933	38	47	34	119	130	249
1934	35	24	130	189	331	520
1935	43	32	330	405	361	766
1936	48	78	401	527	650	1177
1937	46	142	284	472	601	1073
1938	29	83	423	535	704	1239
1939	36	89	447	572	542	1114
1940	5	88	196	289	276	565
1941	–	9	23	32	44	76
Totals	390	811	2268	3469	3756	–

Overall total Weymann and Metro-Cammell total over the above period 7,225

Note. MCW was formed in July 1932 but the precise numbers of bodies built that year that had been ordered through the new regime is unknown – probably not many. In general, the figures are intended to relate to the date of build, though in some cases vehicles were not registered until the following year for various reasons.

Manchester's Other Transit System

Manchester was a reluctant trolleybus operator, as DAVID THROWER recalls

Brand-new and looking every inch a design classic is this fine Crossley TDD6, no.1052 of 1938, resplendent in Manchester's prewar streamline livery. It is posed outside the entrance of the new Rochdale Road depot.

Photos: Greater Manchester Transport Society, except as stated

A rear view of another vehicle, no.1001, the second of the 1938 batch of TDD4s. The trolleybus seems to be almost new but to have entered traffic or be out on test. Note the experimental skate-type overhead pick-up and also the soap advertisement in the rear lower-saloon window, another relatively unusual feature.

THINK OF MANCHESTER TODAY AND YOU think of its smart and efficient Metrolink, now with a decade of service to its credit. And retired Mancunians in their seventies or eighties will gleefully point out that Manchester originally possessed a tram system when they were in their youth, and that it should never have been scrapped in the first place. History, for that particular generation, has now come full circle.

But Manchester once had yet another transit system of sorts. Granted, it ran on tyres rather than rails, and only

mainly served the eastern and north-eastern quadrants of the city. But it was smooth, silent and convenient. It was, of course, the trolleybus network that the transport department operated between 1938 and 1966.

The interior of no.1006, another Crossley TDD4, when still fairly new. Smart moquette, including on the backs of seats, and bulkhead mirrors add touches of refinement, but the bare bulbs add a spartan note.

The lack of enthusiasm by Manchester for its trolleybuses might be said to have been shared across the whole of the north west of England. There were early pioneering systems at Stockport, Wigan and (bizarrely) Ramsbottom, and even a short-lived route in Oldham, and later rather more long-lasting networks at St Helens, South Lancs and Ashton. But there was no real champion with the enthusiasm of Bradford, Newcastle or Bournemouth. Manchester's trolleybus system, something of an unwanted child from the outset, was nevertheless the largest in the region. Today, it is all but forgotten, except by a few.

Origins

The fortunes of Manchester's system are interlinked with those of its smaller neighbour, Ashton-under-Lyne, and so perhaps the story should start there. Lying a few miles to the east, Ashton had been an early user of trolleybuses. The first had been introduced in August 1925, replacing trams on a route between the town and Oldham, via Hathershaw, on the Ashton/Oldham boundary. The route was a joint one with Oldham Corporation. To work the route, Ashton purchased eight Railless/English Electric single-deckers with Short B38C bodies, with Oldham taking two more.

Somewhat curiously, Oldham then turned against trolleybuses due to the noise of their solid tyres

rumbling over stone setts, and so their section of the route, between Hathershaw and Oldham reverted once more to tramcars. Ashton, however, persevered with trolleybuses south of Hathershaw, overcoming their vibrations by fitting the vehicles with pneumatic tyres. One Oldham vehicle was later cannibalised for parts and the other became derelict, but Ashton's early single-deckers lasted until 1937/8.

Ashton's enthusiasm for trolleybuses was then boosted by the local trial of Crossley's first trolleybus, on the Ashton wiring in 1936. It eventually therefore purchased three Leyland TB4s, a Crossley TDD4 and three Crossley TDD6s, which included the demonstration vehicle, all during 1937/8, replacing the early Railless vehicles.

Meanwhile, to the west, Manchester's entry into trolleybus operations was a decidedly controversial and discordant one. It is a story in itself, and so only a summary is given here. In 1935, the full city council rejected their own transport committee's proposals that Manchester's tramcars on the services along

Ashton Old Road should be replaced with motorbuses, and instructed the operating department to continue tramway operation whilst trolleybus powers were obtained through Parliament. When these were obtained in 1936, the council pressed ahead with the introduction of trolleybuses, in the face of continued opposition from the transport committee.

This was an extremely unusual circumstance, and it remains one of the most historic controversies in municipal transport history. But in 1937, the transport committee at least conceded that it would be logical to also convert the Ashton New Road services (for non-Mancunians, Ashton Old Road and Ashton New Road run parallel between Manchester and Ashton), and so the initial order for 43 vehicles was increased to 76. To house this large fleet, a new depot was constructed on Rochdale Road, a few minutes' walk from the eastern edge of the city centre.

In March 1938, Manchester therefore introduced its trolleybuses on the Manchester-Ashton Old Road-Ashton-Stalybridge corridor routes 28/29/29x, the new services being jointly operated with both Manchester's and Ashton's vehicles. In July, trolleybus operations were extended by Manchester and Ashton on the Piccadilly-Ashton Old Road-Audenshaw (Snipe Inn) route 28x. The Piccadilly-Ashton Old Road-Ashton-

Stalybridge route was later renumbered the 218 in early 1950.

Also in July 1938, the former tram route from Manchester via Ashton New Road was converted to trolleybuses, becoming the 27/27x. These, too, terminated at Audenshaw (Snipe). These routes were later renumbered 215/215x in 1950. A further conversion in July was the former 26B/28 tram routes, which became the 26 trolleybus service, Stevenson Square-Ashton New Road-Ashton-Stalybridge. This, too, was later renumbered, becoming the 216 in 1950.

Next, in October 1939, route 29, a former motorbus route, was converted to trolleybuses. This operated from Piccadilly, again via Ashton Old Road, to Guide Bridge. Services initially commenced to the latter destination, but were later extended eastwards in March 1940 to Ashton, where they linked up with the other Old Road services. The services via Guide Bridge were later renumbered 219/219x in 1950, and some journeys on the former 29x became numbered 212 and used Aytoun Street, the roadway that today carries Metrolink from Piccadilly Gardens to Piccadilly Station.

Incidentally, the original Ashton Corporation route, to Hathershaw, was ironically abandoned in favour of motorbuses in February 1939, a victim of Oldham's decision not to develop its trolleybuses, and because a through route between the towns was necessary, rather than enforcing a trolleybus/bus changeover for passengers at Hathershaw.

The next route to be introduced was the conversion of former tram service 57. The new route, also numbered 57, was from Ashton town centre southwards to Denton, commencing in July 1940. In December 1940, it was extended further south to new housing at Haughton Green. The route was later renumbered 217 in the 1950 renumbering scheme. The service was a joint Manchester/Ashton operation because part of the route lay within the Manchester boundary.

The sparkling new Manchester trolleybus fleet that was ordered for these new routes included some very stately vehicles (perhaps all 1930s trolleybus designs were stately?). Certainly, the large batch of prewar trolleys were a design classic, with their distinctive streamline livery.

The first batch to be delivered, in 1938, was numbered 1000-27 (DXJ 951-78). These were two-axle Crossley TDD4s, basically comprising a modified motorbus chassis but fitted with MetroVick motors and with Crossley bodywork constructed upon Metro-Cammell framing. These seated 54 passengers, and featured the extremely attractive white streamline 'swoops' on their vermilion bodysides, with beading lined in mid-brown. They were allocated to the new Rochdale Road depot.

These were accompanied by nos. 1028-37 (DXJ 979-88), a batch of two-axle Leyland TB4s, which were fitted again with Crossley bodies to the same style as 1000-27. Electrical equipment on these was again MetroVick. These, too, went to Rochdale Road.

The third of the 1938 batches was 1050-61 (DXJ 989-93, ENB 175-81), three-axle Crossley TDD6s with 68-seat Crossley/Metro-Cammell bodywork to the same streamlined design as the two-axle batches. These too had MetroVick electrical bodywork. Because of road clearances, these three-axle leviathans could not be used on services where there were sharp corners. Allocated to Rochdale Road, they therefore saw less service than their shorter counterparts.

The last of these initial deliveries was the 1062-87 batch (ENB 182-207), three-axle Leyland TTB4s with similar 68-seat Crossley/Metro-Cammell bodies and again with MetroVick equipment. Like the 1050-61 batch, these too could not be used on routes with tight clearances. These four batches provided a 76-strong fleet to operate the prewar network.

In addition to all these fine new vehicles, the transport department purchased three tower wagons in 1937, mounted on Thornycroft chassis, to augment their existing superannuated fleet of ancillary vehicles. These were to become A114-6 in the service fleet.

Wartime brought further expansion, although it also initially led to the disruption of the existing programme of planned extensions. The Hyde Road route was to have been converted to trolleybuses on 3 September 1939, which of course transpired to be the very day that war was declared. This would have been a joint operation with the SHMD Board, the latter having been on the point of ordering new vehicles. In the event, SHMD was fated never to become an owner of trolleybus vehicles, although it owned its overhead supply.

From April 1940, there was a further new Manchester trolleybus route, this time from the city centre to the university. This was a break away from the eastern corridors already served, and created a short route, numbered 30, southwards from Rochdale Road via the city centre, Ardwick Green and the university, terminating in New York Street. It replaced former tram services 51 and a subsequent temporary bus service. It was renumbered 213 in 1952.

North-eastwards

Next to see trolleybuses was the route from Manchester Church Street along Rochdale Road to Moston. This, the former bus route 55, retained its number and commenced service in November 1940. The reason for conversion was that wartime oil shortages meant that it was now strategically advantageous to prolong the tramway services on the Hyde Road corridor, rather than convert these to trolleybuses, and to divert the new trolleybuses that had already been ordered to replace motorbuses elsewhere.

As former tram poles still stood on Rochdale Road, conversion from buses to trolleybuses was a viable option, and wiring-up the overhead and providing poles, where needed, was accomplished in a bare five months. Incidentally, poles on other routes such as Manchester-Cheetham Hill were left standing for possible future re-use by trolleybuses.

The Moston route via Rochdale Road was extended to Ben Brierley early in 1941. Manchester incidentally seemed to like confusing its passengers by renumbering its routes, and the services became 32/60x in that year. The route was also extended to Nuthurst Road, New Moston, in July 1941, and the corridor's routes were later renumbered yet again, to the 212/212x/214 group of routes, in 1953.

Next, conversion of the parallel Oldham Road route to Moston, which became trolleybus route 37, was authorised, the route being energised in July 1941, with approval only being granted under emergency powers, later retrospectively ratified after the war. This route joined the earlier Rochdale Road route at Ben Brierley, and then extended onwards to Nuthurst Road, New Moston. The new route extended further

Manchester no.1153, a Crossley TDD4 of 1941 and withdrawn in April 1959, is seen in Portland Street in its final month.

to Moston Gardeners Arms in August 1941. A further extension was made in August 1943 from Gardeners Arms to the strategic A V Roe aircraft factory, discreetly termed 'Greengate' on destination blinds. The routes along this corridor, having been renumbered in 1941 and again in 1948, became the 211/211x in 1953.

All these north-eastern sector routes were, of course, exclusively worked by Manchester vehicles. To operate the additional services, and to cope with growing demand, a further batch of 37 Leylands was purchased in 1940, 1100-36 (GNA 18-54), these being two-axle TB5s with MetroVick electrical equipment and Preston-built English Electric 54-seat bodies. These joined the prewar fleet at Rochdale Road, but for some reason two of the batch, 1104 and 1133, later became separated from the remainder and ended their days at Hyde Road.

In addition, during 1940-3, a further 40 vehicles arrived, fleetnumbers 1137-76 and registered GNA 55-94, bringing the fleet strength to a very respectable 153 vehicles. These followed the pattern of previous deliveries and again had Crossley bodies and MetroVick equipment. Most were based from the outset at Hyde Road, though they did not see use on the Gee Cross route. With hindsight, such operating idiosyncrasies seem odd today, and one wonders why the department did not simply standardise on two-axle Crossleys and then use them indiscriminately on all routes.

Meanwhile, to the east, expansion and wartime

traffic demands also resulted in Ashton Corporation's eventual acquisition of six Sunbeam W-type double-deckers during 1944/5.

Postwar expansion

Even after the war, the trolleybus was still seen as playing an important part in Manchester's public transport network. The first postwar extension was of the University route, southwards to Moss Lane East (Moss Side), in January 1946, then to Platt Lane, on the Rusholme/Fallowfield boundary, the following month. This was very new territory for trolleybuses, and might have optimistically, but erroneously, been taken to presage a more general future push into the lucrative tree-lined suburbs of South Manchester. It was a great pity that this was not to occur, for the latter area would have made excellent trolleybus territory, with its scope for services running outwards on radial roads, looping round and returning via a different radial.

To assist in overhead maintenance, Manchester also ordered two further Thornycroft ancillary vehicles. These took several years to be delivered, one finally arriving in 1947 as a tower wagon and numbered A118, and the other in the event being bodied as a van and

switched to other uses. Two further tower wagons, Guy Otters, also later arrived in 1957.

The largest postwar expansion of the Manchester system was the introduction of trolleybuses along Hyde Road. This was an unusual conversion for its time, with the routes converting first from elderly tramcars to diesel buses and only reconverting to trolleybuses after nearly two years. This was due to delays in receipt of new trolleybuses, itself aggravated by acute postwar materials and power shortages.

The new route, numbered 210 and becoming a trolleybus operation from January 1950, was from Piccadilly to Denton and then to Hyde, finally turning southwards to Gee Cross. East of Hyde, it replaced bus route 106. As with the Stalybridge route via Ashton, the destination of this route actually lay within the boundary of the Stalybridge, Hyde, Mossley & Dukinfield Joint Board, and also crossed the Ashton-Haughton Green route 57 at Denton Crown Point. As noted, the SHMD Board was responsible for installation of the overhead supply on the Hyde/Gee Cross section of route.

To cope with booming postwar demand, yet more trolleybuses were ordered by Manchester, these being a batch of two-axle Crossley Empire TDD42/1s with standard-style postwar Crossley bodies seating 58 passengers, and once again with MetroVick equipment. The batch was numbered 1200-37 (JVU 707-44). These were primarily purchased for the Hyde route 210, and were therefore of course based at

Hyde Road garage. Livery was the smart postwar standard, with cream band and cream around the upper-saloon windows rather than the white swoops of prewar days. An interesting feature was that the roofs were also red, to denote an 8ft-wide vehicle. These weighed in over 8 tons 13cwt (by way of comparison, a contemporary London RT motorbus was about a ton less, with a seating capacity just two passengers fewer).

The next batch of trolleybuses to arrive, in 1950, was even heavier still. This was numbered 1240-55 (JVU 745-60), and comprised three-axle Crossley Dominion TDD64/1s with all-Crossley 66-seat bodywork. They were a hefty 10 tons 3cwt, and were always allocated to Hyde Road garage. They seemed to be less popular than other types, and were not scheduled for all-day use, although they did come into their own during the Suez crisis in 1956/7, when trolleybus use was maximised to conserve diesel stocks.

Meanwhile, in Ashton, five more Crossleys with H30/28R bodies also followed in 1950, these becoming numbered 77-81 (LTC 771-5) in the Ashton fleet, Four of the Ashton wartime Sunbeams were also rebodied, the remaining two going to Bradford Corporation.

An excellent posed view of the first BUT/Burlingham to be delivered, no.1302. It arrived three months ahead of the rest of the batch, to iron out any possible faults, and is seen here in sparkling condition at the Gardener's Arms, New Moston, in June 1955. This area was never worked regularly by these vehicles, and the local residents were reputedly incensed that such fine new vehicles were arriving in the city just as their local routes - which had been worked by elderly vehicles well past their best - were being withdrawn and replaced with less-than-new motorbuses.

Ashton's system remained small, but was heavily-used, with for example no fewer than 11million passengers travelling by trolleybus by the mid-1950s, compared with 19 million passengers by motorbus.

By 1953, the Manchester system was operating at its maximum extent, with a fleet of 193 trolleybuses. In terms of fleet size, this placed Manchester as the fifth largest in the UK, exceeded in that year only by Newcastle and Bradford (each with 204 vehicles), Belfast (221) and of course London's 1,800-plus. The previous year, the transport department had given consideration to the further large-scale conversion of motorbus routes to trolleybuses, but the advantages of conversion were by now finely balanced. Pending any shift in this balance of advantage, it was fatefully recommended that further extensions should be deferred. Manchester's network had reached its high water mark.

A final, 62-strong, batch of Manchester vehicles was ordered in 1953 and mostly delivered in 1955, with the last 15 arriving in 1956. These were 1301-62

(ONE 701-62), being BUT 9612T types with MetroVick running gear and with Burlingham H32/28R bodies, the latter having coachwork of a particularly fine quality and thus ending Manchester's trolleybus purchases on a high note. These solid and attractive vehicles spent almost their whole lives at Hyde Road on routes 213 and 215/216/217/218.

Ashton, too, ordered one final batch of eight trolleybuses, these being 821-828 (YTE 821-8). They were BUT 9612Ts with locally-built Bond H33/28R bodywork, and were delivered between September and October 1956. They replaced the five original 1936/7 Crossley and Leyland vehicles, withdrawn in 1955/6, and four of the 1940-built Crossleys, also withdrawn in 1956. Two others of the 1940 batch, nos.57/59, had already previously gone in 1954, and the remaining two, nos.51 and 54, were not withdrawn until 1960.

There were some trolleybus terminal alterations in the late 1950s in Manchester city centre, in connection with the city's ever-changing traffic arrangements – the latter continue to remain in a perennial state of drastic upheaval to this day. In December 1956 the terminus of route 210 was altered from George Street to outside the Queens Hotel, Piccadilly. The terminus of routes 218/219 was moved in June 1957 from Portland Street (Piccadilly Gardens) to alongside the Queens Hotel. Terminal upheavals were not confined to Manchester, and in May 1959, route 215 was moved from the Snipe (Audenshaw) to nearby Ryecroft Hall. And in November 1959, the Stalybridge terminus of the 216 was moved from Waterloo Road into the bus station.

The scattered trolleybus terminal arrangements in Manchester city centre, and their subsequent alterations, ironically meant that quite a significant network of streets was energised. The initial layout included Stevenson Square, Newton, Portland and Aytoun Streets (passing what eventually became the GMPTE headquarters in the 1970s), and London Road, alongside Piccadilly station. This layout was later extended to include Parker Street, with some trolleybuses circumnavigating Piccadilly Gardens, and also included Shudehill, High Street, Church Street and Swan Street, as well as Miller Street and part of Corporation Street.

The Parker Street/Piccadilly Gardens loop went in 1957. The final rationalised post-1963 layout left wiring only in Oldham, Newton, Portland and Aytoun Streets and down London Road. Most of the city centre thus never saw a trolleybus between 1938 and 1966.

As for the earlier batches of vehicles, the 1938 intake was withdrawn between 1950 and 1956, with the three-axle classes being depleted earlier than the two-axle variants. The 1940/1 intake went between 1954-9, and the 1940-3 batch (the 1137-76s) slowly went for scrap between 1953 and 1960.

Rundown

Despite the optimistic delivery of Manchester's Burlingham and Ashton's Bond vehicles in 1955/6, the climate of opinion was turning firmly against the trolleybus.

As ever, development of the overhead network was impeded by the city surveyor's department, which had opposed extension of wiring into key shopping streets, leaving Manchester's trolleybuses on the periphery of the commercial heart of the city, whereas they would have greatly benefited by being routed across the city centre. The city centre termini were also scattered, giving the trolleybuses a very low profile in comparison with other forms of transport. It was almost as though they were an object of slight embarrassment. Also, cross-city operation depended in part on the views of neighbouring authorities such as Salford, Oldham and Rochdale, where there was no enthusiasm for electric traction.

First for conversion to motorbuses were the routes to the north-east. The Moston route via Rochdale Road was the very first to go, ceasing electric operation in April 1955. The Oldham Road route to Moston Gardeners Arms likewise ceased that August. As ever, the reason for abandonment was an impending double bill for both new vehicles and overhead renewals. There had unfortunately been very long intervals between overhauls for many of the trolleybuses, and time had caught up with their bodywork. Some had already been removed from service and stored.

Withdrawal of the Moston area network also resulted in the closure of Rochdale Road depot to trolleybuses, and its conversion to a bus garage. Additional wiring was installed at the other depot, Hyde Road, to give additional trolleybus garaging for the reduced fleet of about 140 vehicles. But the residual services were still busy, and the Ashton New Road and Old Road corridor routes 215/216 and 218/219 alone still required nearly 90 members of the fleet at peak times.

Next for withdrawal was the Platt Lane route 213, which went in May 1959. Its demise was prompted in part by city centre redevelopment and road alterations, a story that was to become all too common across the UK as highway engineers - who saw their role as liberating the movement of the private car - unsympathetically pushed the trolleybus mode towards an early downfall. The conversion of the 213s ended for ever the potential of capturing any of south Manchester for the trolleybus.

The beginning of the end of the network of joint routes with Ashton came with the abandonment of route 217 from Ashton to Haughton Green, in favour of diesel buses, on 3 July 1960. This was another case of fate conspiring against the trolleybus. In fact, extension of the wiring might have been justified, but it was then decided that the extended route could be economically provided by buses, thus prompting conversion of the entire route.

The capital invested in trolleybuses, however, meant that services nevertheless had to continue for some

years yet. Therefore, in 1961, it was decided that the remainder of the Manchester system should be phased out by 1967, although this decision did not find favour in Ashton, where an earlier changeover would have been preferable.

Next to go was the Hyde Road service 210 to Gee Cross, this ceasing in April 1963. This meant that just four basic routes were left, these being the 215/216 group from Piccadilly to Ashton New Road and either Audenshaw (Snipe) or Stalybridge respectively, and the parallel routes 218 via Ashton Old Road to Ashton/Stalybridge and the 219 via Guide Bridge to Ashton.

The next route for withdrawal on the joint system was the Manchester-Guide Bridge-Ashton route 219, trolleybuses ceasing operating without advance public warning on 10 October 1964, although an enthusiasts' tour was run. Also discontinued in 1964 was night route 215X. Manchester's fleet was now down to the BUT/Burlingham type alone. The older batches of vehicles, the 1949/50 Empires and Dominions went during 1963, whilst the BUTs, which were still barely a decade old, were to go during 1963-6, some having been laid up even before the end of the 219s. There were no takers on the secondhand market, despite their solid bodies being good for at least another decade.

The 218 route was now the sole preserve of Ashton Corporation vehicles after May 1966. Saturday workings by trolleybuses on the 215/216 also ceased, from August.

Incidentally, during these closing years of the system, the remaining depot, Hyde Road, was no longer on the main trolleybus service network, but vehicles going to and from the depot still worked over the wiring via Devonshire Street and Hyde Road, and could carry passengers.

Ironic

Ironically, by the 1960s Manchester's transport problems were really beginning to make themselves felt. Comprehensive urban redevelopment had led to the creation of huge overspill estates, most notably at Wythenshawe, forcing many residents to make long journeys back into the city for work and leisure. The rail system was inadequate, and was actually shrinking. As if in recognition of these shortcomings, and perhaps in acknowledgement of the loss of the trams and trolleybuses, in 1966 there were ambitious plans for a new rapid transit system, including options for monorails, guided rubber-tyre systems, busways and railways, but all these came to nothing.

The city authorities seemed to have overlooked the system they already had. The rundown and closure of the trolleybus system appeared at the very least ill-timed. It could have readily been modernised with new vehicles and priority lanes, and its power supplies upgraded or renewed. And there were numerous urban corridors where it could have been extended, or even routed along reserved streets and central reservations. Most of all, it could have been extended very easily to cross the city centre, connecting Piccadilly with the central business district and with Victoria station, or working around a two-way loop via the major shopping streets.

But, as ever with the history of the British trolleybus, it was not to be, and it was to be a further quarter-century before electric transit returned to Manchester's streets, and then only following prolonged lobbying by the Greater Manchester Metropolitan County Council, the Passenger Transport Executive and the City Council.

Returning to 1964, in the Ashton fleet, fleet no.80, the last working Crossley trolleybus in the UK, was withdrawn and set aside for preservation, the rest of the batch having already been withdrawn in the previous year. This left only two of the rebodied Ashton Sunbeams, 61/2, and the eight Bond vehicles, 82-9, operational for 1965. Both Sunbeams went at the end of that year, and two of the Bond vehicles, 85/9, later succumbed in mid-1966, leaving just six Ashton trolleybuses for the final months of the Manchester and Ashton system for the rest of that year.

The last trolleybus to work through Manchester on route 218 was Ashton no.87, which departed from Piccadilly, accompanied by Ashton no.83 as a duplicate, amidst a small throng at 10.27pm on 30 December 1966. The very last 218x was Manchester no.1302, and the last 216x from the Stevenson Square terminus was worked by nos.1353/4. All over Britain, the lights were going out on the trolleybus systems, 1966 also seeing the end of trolleybuses in Nottingham and Newcastle-upon-Tyne, and with Derby, Glasgow, Maidstone and Wolverhampton also going in the following year.

On 31 December, two farewell tours were run, with preserved Manchester no.1344 and, somewhat inappropriately, Rotherham no.44, after which power was switched off. Dismantling of the overhead by contractors was undertaken during 1967, but poles survived in locations such as Piccadilly, where they carried street lighting until the introduction of high mast lighting in the early 1980s.

Survivors

Just two Manchester trolleybuses and two more Ashton trolleybuses survive, which is remarkably fortunate in the circumstances, bearing in mind the impoverished state of preservation in the early 1960s.

All four vehicles differ, giving a fairly representative selection, though the absence of a Manchester

'You've got a face like the back of a bus' used to be an insult in the late 1950s, but there is nothing unattractive about the rear-end of trolleybus no.1158, a Crossley TDD6 of 1940. It was withdrawn in 1958.

Representing the Ashton fleet, no.80, an all-Crossley Empire trolleybus in Piccadilly, Manchester, in August 1958 with a Manchester BUT/Burlingham at the rear. No.80 is now preserved at Manchester's Museum of Transport.
Michael Dryhurst

streamliner is a very sad gap. One of Manchester's 1952 Crossley three-axle Dominions, no.1250 (JVU 775) was very fortunately rescued and was owned in the early preservation era by the East Midlands Transport Society. It is now fully restored, though not operational, and is on display at the well-known Museum of Transport at Boyle Street, Manchester, less than a mile from the one-time MCTD trolley routes that once ran on Rochdale Road.

Also at Boyle Street is the surviving Ashton Corporation Crossley Empire, no.80 of 1950, it having unfortunately degenerated into a semi-derelict state after initial storage elsewhere. Major bodywork rebuilding has since been carried out at Boyle Street, and eventual completion of this particularly historic vehicle is awaited. Another Ashton vehicle, 1956 BUT/Bond no.87, exists at the East Anglia Transport Museum, Lowestoft, and fortunately this is beautifully restored and in full working order.

The temporarily-closed St Helens Transport Museum includes Manchester no.1344, one of the 1955/6-built batch of BUT 9612T vehicles with that stylish Burlingham bodywork. This was initially owned by the Northern Trolleybus Society, and is now owned by the Museum Society, but has not been used now for many years.

In addition to these four, by some freak of history the solitary postwar Thornycroft Sturdy tower wagon, A118, has also somehow survived intact. It was stored derelict in a hangar at Manchester Airport for many years, covered in dust. I had the dubious pleasure of driving it, under tow and on memorably-soggy tyres, back to the city in the early 1980s, and well recall the smoke from the dragging brakes coming up through the floor whenever we halted at traffic signals. It has since been fully restored at the Manchester Museum.

None of these vehicles can enjoy the opportunity to use (or in the case of A118, maintain) any preserved trolleybus wiring in the north west, as unfortunately there is none, but they still serve as important reminders of Manchester's, and Ashton-under-Lyne's, now-forgotten form of electric transit. **CB**

How ROGER DAVIES kept up to date in the 1960s

IT WAS A REALLY CATCHY SLOGAN.
You could almost hear it being sung, and, in conditions of utmost secrecy, I'll confess I did just that. It was 'Keep up to date, read Buses Illustrated'. It was emblazoned across the back of many of the British Bus Fleets books I'd now accumulated. Today, in the dreadful politically correct times of 21st century Britain, there's probably some system that questions why a young boy from Cardiff would want to know whose buses served Quaking Houses and Vinegar Hill (to crews only, a quote from BBF10, I believe the real name was Holycarside), but in the carefree 1960s no such impediment was present. Having got the snapshot the BBFs afforded – and to this day I can quote from them whilst having no clue what Arriva's concept bus may be – the living tale seemed the logical next step. What's gone and what's new, that is the question. (Shakespeare had some muddled view on this, I reckon he was a train spotter.)

So, I bought one. *Buses Illustrated* number 105, December 1963. I got it home and father took one look and said, 'It's very small, I can get you *Commercial Motor* for that and there's a lot more in it'. Well, he was right, but it wasn't a bus enthusiast thing. He did get them for me and they were wonderful, full of lots of adverts for buses and lorries. I threw them out when we moved house in 1970. What can I say?

Anyway, *BI*105 included a little note that from the next issue it was going to be bigger. That just swayed it; my order went in and and, as they say, the rest is history, I still take its successor *Buses*. Good job I didn't start at 104.

It's funny how you get influenced by things. Places are a good example – you know, it's so famous you just have to go there. I was like that with Torremolinos, took a picture of the town name sign. It wasn't that bad; it was February though . . .

Influence

So those early days had a big influence. The cover picture on *BI*105 was the announcement of the

Morning peak, 19 April 1969, in Gervis Place, Bournemouth. Not just a morning peak, but the last morning peak for trolleybuses. From the next day, all this would be confined to the scrapheap. Look, I wouldn't mind if it was all ancient and clapped-out, but it isn't. The oldest of these buses is 11 years old and BCT was still running motorbuses older than that. It is just too unbelievable for words; how could this be true – but it is. I'll say no more other than these fine machines in the last 24 hours of their existence were nos.283/271/287/272. (Apologies if any got preserved, but you know what I'm getting at.)
Photos: Roger Davies

Less than two weeks later I was in Manchester, which just goes to show how bus enthusiasm used to get you around. Here in Cannon Street is one of the 633 squadron of Leyland PD2s, in this case no.3323, a Northern Counties 61-seat PD2/12 of 1954. BI106 tells me that the wide centre front upstairs pillar is to house the ducting for Northern Counties' patented ventilation system. Manchester seemed to go for high seating capacities. Later they had upright-fronted Orions seating 65, which were rather agreeable, 25 of which, came in 1964. They were obviously the ones that weren't supposed to be front entrance. It's remarkable how bus crews adapt bus designs for their own use and the conductor here has used the halfcab layout in a most appropriate way!

Bournemouth trolleybus closure with a very modern trolley thereon. It just didn't seem possible, and today I still can't believe the local politicians got away with such blatant squandering of public money. Some trolleybus systems, whilst lovely, went in a correct manner. My beloved Cardiff system is a case in point. My research into the operator's centenary and articles on it for *Classic Bus* showed that the system was abandoned when new equipment was needed and when it was no longer a reasonable product. With the exception of one single-deck, most buses put in a reasonable innings and justified the investment made in them. Not so Bournemouth and indeed a number of other systems that had invested heavily like Reading, Huddersfield and Bradford. There surely was – no there definitely was – a case to use equipment until it had made a reasonable return on its investment. So they, and Bournemouth in particular, were crimes.

Bournemouth had other connections. My parents honeymooned there and return visits were popular. We holidayed in nearby Swanage for what seemed like every year (it was probably only two or three) so a pilgrimage was easily possible, particularly as we had the car. And there's a thing: in those pre-Severn Bridge days, to go on holiday we would have to get across the estuary or face a huge drive via Gloucester;

there was a ferry but I recall huge queues. So we would set out early from Cardiff and drive to Severn Tunnel Junction where we would put the car on an open railway wagon. We would settle down in a passenger coach and the whole caboodle would set off to steam through the Severn Tunnel to deposit us in far Pilning before the long slow drive to Dorset.

Today, as an avid user of the Channel Tunnel, I view the freight shuttles with some nostalgia.

Poignant

So those yellow Bournemouth trolleys were part of my youth and the announcement doubly poignant. Particularly as Christchurch and Mudeford were an integral part of said Bournemuthian pilgrimage.

When the end was nigh, 1969, which was when some of Bournemouth's newest and finest were but six years old, I made three very different visits. Firstly, a friend of my father drove for Red & White. Occasionally, he would offer trips and twice I was able to accept. One was to Liverpool, the other to Bournemouth. This gave enough time to have a quick whiz around the town centre and get some trolleybus shots before heading back in one of those strange rounded MW coaches hoping no Inspector would board. I'm not sure what my status was, I certainly wasn't a 'stiff'; this phenomena was a passenger who arrived, unbooked, at a coach and was taken on by the driver who then collected the money

Creep up to the editor, part two. Manchester's delivery of 20 of the hush-hush new Leyland single-decks came as Park Royal-bodied Panther Cubs. Actually rather pretty buses, they turned out to be turkeys and didn't last long. Some did find new homes and former no.75 has become Dodds of Troon DT No.9 by the time of this July 1976 view. Dodds was part of the AA consortium and the bus is at its depot in Troon.

This is a Bristol LWL, but wouldn't have been spied by the young Davies over his sandcastle in Swanage because it's a Hants & Dorset one. It's also been rebuilt with a full front, an exercise a number of folk undertook with halfcab buses with varying degrees of failure. Sorry, but it just loses the classic lines of the type. No.783 is here in June 1966 in the H&D bus station in Southampton. 20 years later, after its purchase and immediate sale by Stagecoach, this bus station became part of bus industry folklore.

in, for example, the gents at a motorway stop. I fell into this category a number of times on Sheffield to London runs (27 shillings and 6 pence worth) but not on said R&W jaunts. So stiff I wasn't, criminal more like . . . And it was in the summer of 1968, but you're not to know.

When the end was a lot nigher, early April 1969, I plotted a jaunt over the Easter holidays to take one

last look at these buses that had such a special place in my memories. A chum, not of the bus fraternity, asked if he could come along. He volunteered his tent to avoid paying for a hotel, which swung it. Our local garage man invented some pretext to keep my Ford Pop in the garage long enough to force my father into loaning me his beloved Austin Cambridge, which, as you know, was registered CMU 598A. Soon, I'll be

Bristol, as we would like to remember it and them. Splendid KSW no.C8231 is here in Marlborough Street three days before the end of 1966. As a city bus, I believe it would have been less than welcome in the bus station of the same name which was the heart of the country area operations. Tilling allowed Bristol this relevant scroll fleetname which even survived into NBC days with the double-N symbol being banished to the 'tween decks. Note also the distinctive fleetnumber plate.

asking questions and if you don't read *Classic Bus* you won't stand a chance. Anyway, off we sped and had a good wallow in the yellow wonders. Again nostalgia kicked in and I suggested Swanage to overnight and a suitable flat bit of land was located. We had a good wallow in Badger beer and it got dark and we couldn't find the flat bit. We found a bit of Dorset that would do and my chum assured me he could put up his tent 'in ten minutes with one hand tied behind my back'. I urged him to use the two and finally we settled down to an uncomfortable night. Day dawned to find us perched perilously at the edge of the cliff with what chummy referred to as 'a sea view all those rich idiots are paying a fortune for'. Bournemouth's trolleys were responsible for my one and only night under canvas, it's a wonder I've ever forgiven them.

Geography

You'll remember from last year's offering (pause to reprimand reader and creep into the editor's good books ... they are all good I hear you cry) that geography had been a chosen subject. Thus I was quickly able to assess that getting to Bournemouth from Cardiff was a lot easier than from Sheffield, hence the Easter holiday trip. On my return to college in Sheffield, imagine my surprise to find that the local enthusiast group was running a trip to the Bournemouth closure using its preserved Bedford OB. So within 10 days I was back amongst the yellow chaps. We travelled overnight and again a non-bus chum

came along for the ride and made a significant contribution. In the middle of the night we got lost near Swindon having made a late stop at the corporation's bus garage. Chum along for the ride hailed from Swindon and guided us back on course. I remember traversing one county accompanied throughout by a Police car. Well, I don't suppose they came across a bus load of hairies in the middle of the night that often. (Blimey, haven't used the term 'hairies' for enthusiasts for years!) We arrived in the early morning before any trolleys were up and about so we had a paddle in the sea then bunged the OB on the Christchurch turntable. Like you do. We learned then that Bournemouth trolleybus crews had a special skill. All of us gave the OB a mighty push and it twirled around about 12 times.

I won't dwell on the closure. It was jolly well done but somehow the sight of all the civic dignitaries being feted after they were responsible for the crime of scrapping so much modern kit was just a bit much. I also have an abiding memory of travelling on a new, shiny Alexander Atlantean replacement as it screamed its way around the dignified streets of the genteel resort. If anywhere suited trolleybuses, it was Bournemouth.

But I'm not talking about Bournemouth. Bigger *BI*106 had a special supplement with virtually the whole issue given over to one operator. Manchester City Transport. Talk about breath being taken away;

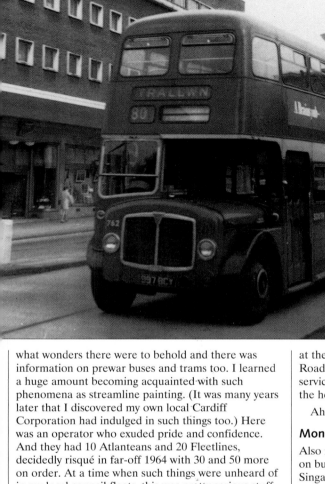

Swansea as I would like to remember it. Well not quite; by this May 1972 view, AEC Regent V no.762 has gained the wishy-washy red of the reorganised company and the rather apologetic fleetname. Still, it's a Regent in Princes Way in central Swansea, so it'll do. I've never really got on with the Willowbrook body that so many SWT Regents had, but it does sum up the fleet nicely. There's also a rather splendid Scammell truck behind.

what wonders there were to behold and there was information on prewar buses and trams too. I learned a huge amount becoming acquainted with such phenomena as streamline painting. (It was many years later that I discovered my own local Cardiff Corporation had indulged in such things too.) Here was an operator who exuded pride and confidence. And they had 10 Atlanteans and 20 Fleetlines, decidedly risqué in far-off 1964 with 30 and 50 more on order. At a time when such things were unheard of in my local council fleets, this was pretty serious stuff. (They also had 75 PD2s and 20 CV6s on order, 50 of the Leylands being forward entrance. Quite, I never saw them either, so here's another example of the lure of our hobby. No doubt they were changed into Atlanteans, very much a sign of those times when rear-engined buses became quickly established in the major fleets.) The total fleet stood at 1,401 made up of 633 Titans, 384 CVs, 233 Crossleys, 66 trolleybuses, and said 30 rear-engine jobs. There were 55 single-decks made up of, wait for it, 14 Tiger Cubs, 35 Royal Tigers and six Albion Aberdonians. And there's more, *BI* asserts that 20 of the as yet 'hush-hush' Leyland single-decks with underfloor engines mounted at the rear were also on order. Just imagine having 195 new buses on order! And doesn't it make you think, those new single-decks were eagerly awaited, it was really exciting stuff, and they were a real sensation when they arrived. One, no.62, now a not so hush-hush Panther Cub, was

at the 1964 Earls Court show along with a Daimler Roadliner. The first production Bristol REs entered service at that time too prompting *BI*116 to lead with the headline 'A New Generation of Single Deckers?'

Ah, if we had known then what we know now . . .

Monster

Also interesting is that during 1964, *BI* carried articles on buses in Spain, Rhodesia, Aden, Ceylon, Malaya, Singapore and Sarawak, so there was global interest even then. But back to *BI*106 which also included an article on bus preservation, an entirely new concept to me, entitled 'FUF, our green and cream monster'. It was written by one Thomas W W Knowles, who in later years I came to know and work alongside. In April it carried an article on Cardiff's single-deck trolleybuses – so that was it, I was hooked. If all that wasn't enough, the December edition cover picture was of an Edinburgh PD3 taken by one Gavin A Booth. Wonder what the A stands for . . .

The point I'm making is that in the space of a few months, my knowledge in, and enjoyment of, my hobby grew immeasurably. Those first few operators that were featured held a special place as a result.

Now Swanage, you remember Swanage? There were buses there and they had an impact on the young Davies too. If the clever-clogs will just hang on a mo, I'll say Hants & Dorset. This company, probably more

This rather sums up United Welsh's presence in Swansea ... perhaps a little unfairly! June 1969 finds no.385 in Plymouth Street in less than agreeable surroundings. Do you take my point comparing it with SWT no.762? No.385 is unusual in being an FLF, United Welsh tended to favour the shorter and rarer FSF model.

than Bournemouth, calls up happy holiday memories. Tilling companies were not that well represented in South Wales; we had the quirky Red & White and the rather small United Welsh, both being red. So the green H&D were a refreshing change and went well with Bournemouth's yellow giving the whole area a cheery sort of look. I was particularly impressed by the way H&D's bus stop plates were cream with green edging and letters, as you moved into Wilts & Dorset territory they were the same but in red. The sight of green bus stops meant we were nearly there and the holiday with weeks of glorious sunshine lay ahead. Well, it did then, didn't it?

Incidentally, I once wrote a piece for English at school which introduced a smart independent operator's bus that was, I quote, 'a change from the usual green or red Tilling companies'. This elicited a large red query from the English master. I forgave him, he introduced me to 'Lord of the Rings'.

OK, it's your turn, clever-clogs, because they weren't H&D in Swanage, they were Western National. This was a delightful little bit of history that Tilling clearly saw no reason to change. NBC did, and a lot of these anachronisms that added to the interest were swept away. More's the pity. I'm still not convinced that there was that much to be gained in all cases. Anyway, Swanage's front was graced by Bristol LWLs with roof-mounted boat racks, and, yes, I've yet to find out why.

Swanage's front was also graced by two sisters from Bristol. Clearly some bond or other was forged as we later visited them at home in that city. Thus I came to know Bristol Omnibus. Cardiff and Bristol actually

have quite close ties and at the risk of upsetting those with a Welsh leaning I would maintain that those ties are much more relevant than, say, ones with Caernarfon or Aberystwyth. (Note to Plaid Cymru: Look guys, my car already is green, so there's no need to trouble yourselves). We used to get the West Country version of the BBC local news so I was well up on things like the Bath & West Show. When the Severn Bridge opened in 1966, it brought to an end the car train and ferry services but R&W and Bristol introduced a joint bus service between the cities which brought green Tillings into Cardiff. Early in 1967 a Bristol RE bus turned up on the 301 and there was something about it. I couldn't work it out and stared and then studied my photo of it. It had got a flat front, the first I'd seen. Now my enthusiasm for things Bristol/ECW is not that great, but I always felt the first RE body was a bit of a classic and looked particularly fine in green. The flat front was a retrograde step in my view. Said R&W driver (remember him?) claimed that in strong winds the flat-fronted REs were almost brought to a stop on the bridge whilst the rounder ones weren't. Mind you, he was a bit of a card.

Big city

Bristol always seemed to have the feel and excitement of a big city about it. We used to go tenpin bowling there, Cardiff not being equipped with such delights. The railways did a super offer in the evenings, 7s 6d return, which made it a popular night out. First heard 'Hello Goodbye' there . . .

And Bristol Omnibus. Here was a major

Yes, and independents. South Wales rejoiced in many and Brewers of Caerau was particularly interesting as it tended to follow the major fleets in its new bus purchases. A microcosm of the majors in fact, even here to being arguably ahead of one, SWT. Western Welsh had this style of body on Leopards, but SWT hadn't got it on Reliances such as this, their first having curved BET style screens. So Brewers 278 TNY was pretty well cutting-edge when it was new. I've also a feeling it was Weymann rather than Willowbrook, but you lot out there can put the record straight, no doubt. Its here in Lawrenny Avenue, Cardiff in October 1969 providing transport for Cardiff City fans. (Football, not buses, fatheads . . .)

conurbation served by a company operator using buses you were more used to seeing wandering about on country lanes (or sea fronts). It was odd. Despite being standard rather dull Tilling kit, there was an individuality about it like the embossed fleetnumber plates and high fleetnumbers. There was also the interest of all the different fleets and even the different livery in Cheltenham. Despite being apparently one, the demarcations between each fleet were very clear and strong, which I suspect helped foster pride in the job. It always was a special fleet, and it is surprising how many retired people I know from the industry that worked there. It was also amongst the favoured few that had their own BBF, in Bristol's case, number 13.

So Bristol was an early influence. Another was South Wales Transport. In a way this was the BET equivalent, a company operator serving a large town, Swansea (it wasn't a city then). Both places also

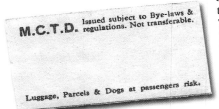

BOURNEMOUTH CORP. TRANSPORT

ISSUED SUBJECT TO BYE-LAWS & REGS.

Ticket time. Bournemouth favoured both Ultimate (page 121) and Setright, I expect on crew and driver only respectively. Manchester had very formal MCTD Setrights; there's an unused one on the right. Most interesting of all, a Bristol Ultimate, most likely from the City fleet and unusual for a Company fleet, can be seen on page 122.

M.C.T.D. Issued subject to Bye-laws & regulations. Not transferable.

Luggage, Parcels & Dogs at passengers risk.

had their own distinctive registration series. I suppose I took it as the norm that local buses were run by the council, so this was unusual. But what a fleet! BET dark red comes in for a bit of criticism but I found it a businesslike and confident livery on SWT buses, particularly when it sported a cream band below the windows. But it was the buses that did it for me, great hordes of varied AECs; it couldn't have been more different from Bristol. I felt sorry for the few local folk who had to put up with Lodekkas from United Welsh when there were all these Regents and Renowns tearing around. United Welsh even seemed out of it by having a dingy little bus station in a back street whilst the Regents stalked commandingly along the wider avenues of the rebuilt town centre. I've always had a bit of a soft spot for so-called 1960s architecture, I suppose it was because it was new when I was young and old buildings tended to be dirty. Anyway, that's how I prefer to remember Swansea.

Getting there was part of the adventure. You could travel in style on the Neath & Cardiff 'brown bombers' or go by train which afforded such delights as a view of Western Welsh's Port Talbot depot which on one trip housed the first withdrawn Weymann Tiger Cub of the massive fleet of 180 the company had amassed. Unfortunately, the train entered Swansea via what was at the time described as the largest area of industrial dereliction in

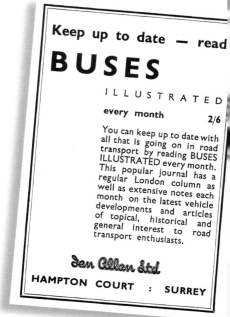

The cover of new enlarged *BI*106 features Manchester CVG6 no.4584 sporting the attractive Manchester-style front. The caption notes that MCW's standard shell, opening vents and destination gear make it distinctive – another example of the variety of our hobby in those days. My victory was quite quick, the '19 V West' in the corner was our address so it was delivered by the local newsagent. Note the Crossley trolley and Burlingham PD2 in the background.

Britain and was just a bit grim. Say it as I shouldn't, the best way was by car. You queued your way through Port Talbot savouring the splendid blue Thomas Bros fleet and then the excitement really started. Over the Briton Ferry bridge you may catch the first glimpse of an imposing red AEC on the way from the seaside resort of Aberavon. I recall some (I'm pretty sure it was just Bridgemasters) having a red warning triangle on the back advising they were fitted with air brakes. Whatever, some of my Matchbox double-decks gained the same feature. Then the run along wild and open Jersey Marine before entering the town via industrial areas near the docks. Yes, all fine and dandy, but the buses were all part of it, identifiable with it, special to it and I recall it all with fondness. Nowadays, presumably, both cities have the same buses in the same colour, I don't know, I've never been to look.

Independents

Now, you may have noticed that all the fleets I've mentioned have been part of the main groups, BET, Tilling or municipal. And, yes, it is true that I tended that way, maybe because the BBFs in general listed such fleets. This was despite South Wales being very well endowed with independent operators. *BI* changed

that, within months I had absorbed a delightful dissertation on Burwell & District and another on Pennine of Gargrave. Eleven years later, I was privileged to work jointly with the latter, but it did involve an exceedingly draughty site meeting in a blizzard that I would rather forget. I also read of Moore's of Kelvedon, absorbed by Eastern National about a year previously. The article was entitled '12 months Moore or less' which I found very neat. Recklessly, I quoted it to family and friends as evidence that bus enthusiasm had its funny side. Bad move. Anyway, I am plotting a piece on independent operators wot I have known, all as a result of those early days with *BI*.

I had lots of good times and visited many places, getting to know the UK very well in the process, in pursuit of buses. Much of that is down to those pioneering spirits who wrote for *BI* and compiled the BBFs and, belatedly, thanks to you all. I'd like to think my aimless ramblings could do the same, but as all you'll find is a Pointer Dart or an Envirothingy, I'm not too hopeful.

Still, you could always try singing the slogan ... all together now ... 'Keep up to date, dah dee dah dee dah, read Buses Illustrated!' **CB**